Des Lynam

Des Lynam

The Biography

STEVE PURCELL

André Deutsch

First published in 1999
by André Deutsch Limited
76 Dean Street
London W1V 5HA

www.vci.co.uk

A catalogue record for this book is available from the British Library

ISBN 0 233 99661 3

Typeset by Derek Doyle & Associates, Liverpool
Printed in the UK by Mackays of Chatham

Contents

Acknowledgements

My heartfelt thanks to the many people who have contributed towards this celebration of a unique broadcasting talent, but especially to: Bob Wilson, the former Arsenal and Scotland goalkeeper and for so long a friend and rival to Des; to Stanley Allen and John Henty for their reminiscences of radio days gone by; *Match of the Day Magazine* for help and assistance; Brian Barwick, former Head of Sport at the BBC; Gerry Williams; Terry Venables; Susan Lynam; Laura Ewing; Paddy Brennan for sharing his childhood memories; and to the many others who do not need to be named for them to know how much I appreciate their help.

Foreword

As a typical sport-obsessed male I was delighted to be asked to write a biography of Desmond Lynam – a man who has been 'a mate' to millions of us fanatical football followers for as long as I care to remember.

There's been *Match of the Day*, of course, the highpoint of any Saturday night for the last ten or fifteen years, and *Sportsnight* where Des would guide us through the midweek news and events in his typical laid-back style. And then there was *Grandstand* on Saturdays and occasional Sunday afternoons where I remember Des and, before him, the greats such as David Coleman and Frank Bough keeping us up to date with the unfolding dramas of weekend sport.

So I was, and remain, a fan of not just the sports like soccer and tennis from Wimbledon, but of the man who brings them to us with calm assurance, and a wit and style which helps us not only to appreciate the sport, but also its place in the greater scheme of things.

Des has one of the most recognizable faces in British broadcasting. The consummate professional. With his easy charm, sparkling humour and handsome good looks he has captivated millions of fans both male and female, sporting and non-sporting.

But he is also a famously private individual, jealously guarding his life away from the cameras. When he first hit the 'big time' he became known as the Garbo of *Grandstand*.

He transcends the barriers of age and class. As someone pointed out, perhaps it takes an Irishman to become the ultimate classless voice of the British broadcasting establishment.

As his reputation grew within the BBC, so too did his reputation outside it as 'a ladies' man'. Comedienne Caroline Aherne, in her role as Mrs Merton, famously called him a 'Tom Cruise for menopausal women'. But what do the women who have shared his life think of the man we love to call Dishy Des?

He has covered World Cups, Olympic Games, Wimbledon tennis and, of course, the Grand National during a career spanning some thirty years. But did you know that his first love was boxing?

Writing this book has been something of a labour of love. When I first began to look at Desmond's life, I was astonished to find that, like mine, his father came to England from Ireland after the Second World War. Mine from Kilkenny, his from Ennis. Both our fathers died prematurely from illness rather than old age; something which appeared to have affected us both deeply. Like Des, I went to the local grammar school but turned my back on a university place because of the financial implications for my parents. Like him, I started out in local journalism, although Des had a stab at selling insurance first, married and divorced while progressing up the career ladder, and, like Des, I had a son called Patrick from marriage to a girl called Susan. (I also had a daughter, Jennifer.)

So, those coincidences made the project even more fascinating for me. But it has not been without its share of heartache. Discovering the fine detail about Des has not been an easy task. You have no idea how many phone calls, faxes and repeated conversations it takes to pull together just one anecdote.

Let me just say that I'm very grateful to those close to Desmond Michael Lynam who have helped me to compile this biography – this tribute – to the best broadcaster of his time. Some, like Brian Barwick his former boss at the BBC who pulled off the transfer deal of the decade when he persuaded Des to sign for ITV, would argue the best ever.

And finally, thanks are due to my wife Jane for her support and encouragement and to my children Kitty and Harry who made me laugh when I wanted to scream!

1

Our Summers with Des

If you can talk with crowds and keep your virtue,
Or walk with kings – nor lose the common touch;
If neither foes nor loving friends can hurt you;
If all men count with you, but none too much;
If you can fill the unforgiving minute
With sixty seconds' worth of distance run –
Yours is the Earth and everything that's in it,
And – which is more – you'll be a Man, my son!
                                        'If', Rudyard Kipling

It was the summer when football came home – a summer of blue skies, endless optimism and singalong euphoria. England had known nothing like it since 1966, a full thirty years before, when the rest of the world came to pay homage at the 'home' of football; and were taught the lesson that they deserved as the game's founding fathers became the World Champions for the first and only time.

The patriotic fervour of a nation denied such glory ever since had not only been rekindled, it burned brighter than ever as the big stars of the modern game arrived for the European Championships, the world's second most important soccer tournament.

People who professed a hatred of soccer suddenly found themselves assessing the chances of Croatia in Group D; or discussing the merits of the Dutch sweeper system as opposed to the use of wing backs to attack the flanks. A year before they

1

wouldn't even have been able to tell you that football is a game of two halves, mate. They might just about have heard of Wembley, though: it's a suburb in north London. Take the Bakerloo or Jubilee lines on the Underground, OK!

But now mothers, wives, lovers, girlfriends – even the most football-allergic of the female sex – knew what time the next big England match kicked off. Football had become the new religion, and every day thousands of new followers took heed of the message from its apostles – those superstar players who right through the 1990s had been taking over from Hollywood's cinematic heart-throbs as the new all-action heroes of a generation.

And there, at its centre, an oasis of calm in a vortex of hysterical emotion was Desmond Michael Lynam.

In that dramatic, and eventually heartbreaking, summer of 1996 Des Lynam found himself inextricably woven into our national fabric.

The BBC's smooth anchorman, known by the affectionate sobriquet of the 'Silver Fox', crossed the great divide between mere television sports presenter and becoming a household name, an international televisual sporting icon, a great British institution even. He became as familiar to housewives as he was to the sporting anorak, vacuum-sealed in his fact-lined bedroom; as much a part of the family as Captain Birdseye. And, as John Motson might have put it, 'like Moses parting the Red Sea, he walked it'. In fact, later in the year Des did part the Red Sea – albeit in an hilarious send-up of his new iconic status in an advertisement for Right Guard deodorant.

This was the summer when a visitor from space could have been forgiven for thinking that our television sets were nothing more than a vehicle for bringing one middle-aged, insomniac, sports-mad preacher into our living rooms. There was the usual tennis from Wimbledon; a lavish Olympic Games from Atlanta and, more importantly, three weeks of football in our own backyard. All of it presented by Des.

And instead of getting celebrity fatigue, Des just became more familiar. We expected to see him. Wanted to.

Actress Rachel Weisz, who later featured opposite Neil

Morrissey in a television play about Des and his God-like role in our lives during Euro 96, captured the essence of why he appeals to more than just die-hard sports fans, saying: 'Des is more charismatic than practically any actor I've ever come across. He's got real movie star eyes and that slow-burn, smouldering quality. I think he would be very good in a leading role. The main thing you need in films is charisma and he really has it without trying. He's got pots of it.'

After weeks of hype and build-up, appetites well and truly whetted, the nation was welcomed to Euro 96 with a classic piece of Lynam mischief: 'Hello, it's June the thirtieth. We're at Wembley for the 1996 European Championship final, England against Scotland . . . ' It was actually 8 June and the opening day of the European Championships, when England were due to play Switzerland before an expectant capacity crowd. But with a glint in his eye and the trademark raising of one of those bushy eyebrows he added: 'Well, we can all dream, can't we?'

It was the kind of thing your best mate might have said; delivered with an irresistible impishness which women find so appealing. In one telling moment he had endeared himself to both parties in the household.

It was also the kind of line which, subsequently, attracted the comedian and playwright Arthur Smith's attention and altered the course of history for them both.

Long after English hearts were broken by the outstretched arms of a goalkeeper in the semi-final penalty shoot-out against Germany; long after the Germans had gone on to lift aloft the glittering prize at Wembley, making up for their heartache of three decades ago; Smith sat down to write a television screenplay. It had started out as *An Evening with Gareth Southgate*, after the villain of the piece in that dramatic semi-final penalty shoot-out which followed an agonizing period of extra time against Germany.

Southgate, as everyone who watched the game will never forget, smashed the ball against German 'keeper Andreas Kopke from the penalty spot in the first of the sudden death spot kicks. With five penalties scored by each side in the shoot-out, Southgate's vital miss allowed Andreas Moller to deliver the killer blow to England's hopes by crashing the ball into the roof of David Seaman's net. Just as they had done six years earlier in the 1990 World Cup, England had lost out to Germany after 120 minutes of open play had failed to separate the two old adversaries. Collectively the nation sank to its knees or buried its head into cupped hands and groaned in disbelief.

That night, back in the BBC studio, Des delivered another of his little gems, commenting: 'There we are. No use crying for what might have been. Not for more than a couple of years anyway.' It was another line which mightily impressed Smith, who had a huge hit with his earlier play *An Evening with Gary Lineker*. The more research he did for his new play, scouring coverage of Euro 96 for little nuggets, the more it became apparent that the biggest star of the tournament had been not England's top scorer Alan Shearer or Germany's Jurgen Klinsman, but the BBC's consummate link-man who was a constant factor throughout the entire proceedings – Des.

Smith recalls:

'I was rung up by the *Independent* newspaper after we got knocked out of Euro 96 by the Germans to do a story. When it went out the BBC phoned up and asked did I want to turn it into a screenplay. The piece was to be a romantic comedy played out against the backdrop of this great football festival which was four weeks of joy, disappointment and tension – like a brief intense love affair.

'At that point I think I only mentioned Des briefly, as a figure to be admired. There was one line about him, I think.

'I was determined, though, to have quite a lot of clips about football trailing all the way through, so I had to watch Euro 96 again as part of my research. I wanted the rhythm of the football tournament to inform the progress of my two lovers and I was looking for moments in the games to punctuate the story.

'The more I watched it, the more I noticed Des would come out with a really funny line, or something quite perceptive – stuff that, for me, really moved the play along. I found myself becoming fascinated by his smooth control and elegant utterances.

'So I started putting little bits of Des in and little bits of Jimmy Hill and Alan Hansen. Somehow Des emerged as this *deus ex machina* type figure, which I had sort of done with Gary Lineker previously in *An Evening with Gary Lineker*. It did seem at that moment, that this was Des's time, Des's moment. He had not got that much publicity before really but in '96 he was everywhere – the European Championships, Wimbledon, the Olympics.

'The play started as *An Evening with Gareth Southgate*, or something, then it was going to be called *My Summer with Rosie* and then, as Des came in more and more, there was this feeling that this was where Des was going to take his bow. Then, as I was writing this, the advert came out with Des as some God-like figure and I thought, "Well, I've caught the zeitgeist here a bit."

'It was as though he had paid his dues and it was "Right, take a bow Des Lynam time". My thing coincided with that sort of feeling.

'Putting Des's name in the title – well you don't need to say Des Lynam do you...? he's a kind of Madonna or something – seemed like a good idea and the BBC were quite keen. It was a good title. People knew what to expect. Suddenly it took on a different life.

'By then I was beginning to write lines for Des – I had him doing quotes from *Hamlet* and all sorts. Naturally it didn't all make the final cut but he certainly became a central character.'

Although the play casts him as this ironic God-like figure, Des was more than happy to 'ham it up' and, very successfully, to show that he doesn't take his own exalted status too seriously. Smith says:

'Des loved the play and he loved playing a part in it. I always wanted to have Des's lines fairly tasteful but he was up for smuttier stuff. I think Des is a bit more racy off screen than he is on. He's a natural really.

'I get the impression with most sports broadcasters that

they live in a cupboard at the back of the studio. They have no life outside sport. Not so Des who looks as though he may once have rescued a beautiful blonde from a tribe of bandits in Patagonia. You could imagine him riding to the rescue of a damsel in distress and carrying her off on a white horse.

'Roguishness is part of his charm. That twinkle in the eye business. There's always the suggestion with Des that he's got a racy background. You don't quite know where he's come from or what he's up to. That somehow he's got this racy past – which in fact he has, it would transpire.

'The fact that he appeals to women is very important. Over the years women who didn't particularly like football will have seen Des on television and felt comfortable with him. There's a familiarity with Des.

'He's been doing this for a long time and there's this sort of cult. There was this "Des is God"' phase. Oddly they chose Des, rather than someone a bit more sexy. He's a middle-aged man – an old man even.

'In a secular age though, Des could be God. Football became a religion and it was looking for a God. But it can't really be one of the players, they are just the apostles. The thought is that the world is manipulated and if there is a God, it must be Des. It's ironic.

'Des has an advanced sense of irony which is lacking in your average sports presenter.'

He certainly does. Des was not at all phased delivering lines like, 'He's a naughty boy but he's a class act.' Or, 'All the teams are arriving here in mostly undamaged aircraft', a reference to the England team's riotous homecoming from Hong Kong just before Euro 96 after the infamous tour of the Far East. Or another classic, 'You know, if you've bought the trunks you have to go swimming.'

In fact, the extraordinary quality of Des's normal verbal links means that in the play, written by a professional comic and author, it's impossible to tell which lines were written by Smith and which ones he's lifted from Des's actual coverage on television.

Des's place in the scheme of things is established early on in Smith's play. Three of the main characters are discussing who is better looking – movie idol Brad Pitt, a real teen fantasy, or Des Lynam. Martin, the football-fixated man who packs in his job to watch Euro 96, played by Neil Morrissey, says: 'Brad isn't in the same league as Des.' His pal's girlfriend adds: 'He's Vauxhall Conference compared to Des.'

The pal, Cameron, studies them both and says: 'I'm trying hard not to like Des Lynam. It's a form of mental exercise. He's got a moustache for God's sake.' But Martin shoots back: 'Des Lynam is God. Everyone knows that.' The exchange ends with a shot of Des looking pensive and rubbing his famous 'tache.

So, it was the play which marked the emergence of Des Lynam as a national figure, but it was the sports-filled summer of '96 which was really responsible for his familiarity. No one turning on their television during that delightful summer could avoid, at some stage, the beaming smile of Mr Cool, bringing the latest from the worlds of soccer, tennis or the Atlanta Olympics like some sport-obsessed insomniac.

When he first came to the attention of Arthur Smith with his bit of whimsy about an England versus Scotland cup final, he was actually introducing the opening game of the tournament featuring England and Switzerland. The opening ceremony was a lavish spectacle with knights on horseback charging around the Wembley perimeter and even a St George slaying a fire-breathing dragon. There were parachute displays and children with colourful flags and an electric party atmosphere.

The only damp squib was the actual game, played out to a rather boring 1–1 draw which somewhat deflated the previously euphoric supporters. The only positive note for England was that Alan Shearer found the net for the first time in almost two years of international competition. Like many curtain-raisers, though, it could surely only be the start of more dramatic things to come.

England's second game, a few days later, brought the Auld Enemy, Scotland, to the three lions' den. In glorious sunshine, a glorious game finally ignited the championships. And there was no one more excited than the BBC commentary team, led of course by Des. The night before the game he urged fans to tune in, saying: 'England versus Scotland. It's there for you tomorrow. We have to go, so see you tomorrow . . . if you're not going to a boot sale or anything.' As if we would.

During the game Shearer proved he was back in business by scoring from Gary Neville's cross then, crucially, David Seaman saved a penalty from Scots' captain Gary McAllister.

As the game instantly swept back downfield, the bewildered Scots were caught out by a surging run from Paul Gascoigne. Showing world-class skill, he flicked the ball over Colin Hendrie before volleying an unstoppable shot past Andy Goram for one of the greatest goals ever scored at Wembley.

Back in the commentary team's room the English contingent erupted with joy. Des himself let out a cry of glee and leapt from his chair. After all the misgivings about Gascoigne and the rowdy behaviour of players in the build-up to the championships, that one piece of supreme skill would have the panel purring with delight for hours.

On 18th June, Wembley was a sea of orange as the pride of Holland arrived. There was a buoyant mood about the England supporters but no one envisaged the stunning display Terry Venables's men would produce that afternoon. It was meant to be a tricky game. Des, Jimmy Hill and the team discussed the mathematics of qualification from the first round to the quarter-final stages because, after all, England had only drawn their opening game. There was nothing to worry about. England crushed Holland 4–1 with one of the best displays seen at Wembley for years.

England were through to face Spain in the quarter-finals but a wave – some, including Des, would say an unfortunate wave – of patriotic fervour swept through the nation. As keen as anyone to give passionate support to the national team, Des hates that mindless yobbery which some small sections of the football-loving public can display. But now it was being manifested in the national press, too. Newspapers took the build-up to a xenophobic extreme.

Naturally, this was not reflected in the calm analysis on the BBC except for Des to comment that things were getting out of hand. Remember that when England had been defeated by Germany in the 1990 World Cup, though bitterly disappointed personally, he famously advised everyone: 'If you go out for a drink tonight, do it with pride, not anger, in your hearts.'

The game against Spain was nail-bitingly close. One hundred and twenty minutes of open play failed to separate the two teams – and the period of extra time involved the new rule of the 'golden goal', meaning the first team to score would win. Finally the game was settled in a penalty shoot-out with Seaman saving one, another Spanish effort hitting the bar and Stuart Pearce, the old English warhorse, burying the bitter disappointment of his own penalty miss against the Germans in Turin six years previously, by coolly hammering his effort home for the winner.

After it all, Des summed up the relief we all felt by saying, 'You can come out from behind your settees now.' Once again, he had perfectly caught the mood of the moment and voiced the relief of 18 million viewers.

The hype and hysteria which preceded the Spanish game was nothing compared to the pressures which surrounded the semi-final, though. It was to be against Germany – always the most accomplished, experienced and difficult of opponents. The newspapers were full of bullish banner headlines and the anticipation for the biggest England versus Germany Wembley clash since 1966 was almost tangible. Everyone seemed to be getting carried away. Everyone, that is, except Des. On 26 June, Des beamed out at just under 20 million viewers and said, casually: 'Glad you've tuned in. You've probably heard there's a football match on tonight.'

It was a prime example of how Des, the master of irony, understates the case to cut the tension and remind people that, hey, it's only sport . . . it's not a matter of life or death.

Earlier he had set the scene by closing coverage of the first semi-final by reminding viewers that the England–Germany game could be seen live on both BBC and ITV. But with a meet-you-down-the-pub-for-a-beer-later look in his eye he told the audience: 'I'd be surprised if you didn't watch it on the BBC. Frankly, I'd be disappointed.' He was right. The BBC trounced

ITV in the ratings, taking 19.8 million of the estimated 26.2 million who tuned in. His great friend and rival, Bob Wilson, over on ITV would relish the moment a couple of years later, however, when his channel scooped the biggest television audience in British history with the England versus Argentina World Cup semi-final.

The game proved to be the epic everyone had expected with Shearer scoring a classic goal just two minutes after the kickoff only for Stefan Kuntz to equalize for Germany. The game went to extra time amid much drama and excitement and then, fatally, it was penalty shoot-out time again.

After five successful penalties each, Southgate stepped up for the split second he'll never forget. And suddenly the dream was over. Des was quick to prepare his 'escape' from the live programme but, as ever, he wanted to exit on a high note rather than a downbeat one. 'Well, I hope you enjoyed it despite the disappointment at home,' he said. 'You'd better remember where you were watching this because in thirty years' time someone will probably ask you.'

So, what is it about Des that sets him apart from other good broadcasters? Why do people like and trust him so much? Smith reckons:

> 'It's partly down to his longevity. And the fact that he's so much better at his job than anyone else. He's at once involved in it like a fan, but detached as well. You know with Des that if something terrible goes on on the pitch that is outside the remit of football, like a bomb goes off, you kind of trust yourself in Des's hands, whereas your average football man would be all at sea.
>
> 'Look at that time the Grand National was abandoned because of a bomb threat. Des has the experience and sensitivity to deal with the situation. On such occasions, when political questions have been considered, your average sports link person may flounder badly and probably end up advocating the return of hanging. Des, one knows, will say the right thing.

'So he's got an air of detachment and you know that in the end he will say that football is not the most important thing in the world, or sport generally. He wouldn't use the word "tragedy" to describe a football team's relegation – not even if it were his own Brighton and Hove Albion, which it often is.

'When there is all this absurd overstatement like, "football is life", Des has a much more mature handle on it. The difference between the BBC coverage and Sky coverage is personified by Des. With Des there's expert talk and amusement but there's still an air of "It's only sport". It's not hysterical.

'Des tends to react to the game rather than impose a kind of excitement on it. Like on Sky they'll say, "Oh, it's Sheffield Wednesday versus Barnsley, what a thrilling encounter. It's out of this world." Des wouldn't do that. Des wouldn't go so far as saying, "Oh God, this is a boring game," but he would hint at that in a way which was agreeable. He's got that authority.'

Des himself admits that, although he loves sport in general, and football and boxing in particular, there comes a time when you have to get it into perspective. He has said: 'Well, it becomes life and death for some people, but in the end it's a bit of fun, isn't it? Having said that, I remember the 1970 World Cup quarter-final, England two up against West Germany. When we lost 3–2, I remember going out later that night and drinking myself on to the floor, and, you know, I wasn't a child at the time. England had such a good team in '70, they could have won the damned thing. They were better than the '66 team that won the World Cup.'

He's a true fan and that's part of his appeal. But if you had to pick out one attribute from Des's winning hand which gives him the edge over the competition it would have to be his sense of humour. Smith agrees.

'Des scores heavily on humour, too. ITV try to do it but it just doesn't come off.

'He is naturally very funny and he's pretty assiduous. Those tossed-off one liners that are really pretty good. They are memorable some of them. My favourite is "There's Frank Leboeuf and his son – le Spare Rib".

'And he has a writer's ability to avoid cliché. In the build-up to Euro 96 I saw a preview in which he said, "Euro 96. It's all about to get under way. The biggest event since . . . Well, you've heard all that stuff." Writing links on TV is hard to do well.'

Des can also turn it on off the top of his head. In old-fashioned soccer parlance, he can swivel on a sixpence before unleashing an Exocet to burst the old onion bag. Smith recalls asking Des if the *Match of the Day* team go out for dinner together. 'Only if we can shake off Jimmy Hill,' quipped Des, before quickly adding that he was only joking and paying fulsome tribute to the man with whom the viewers love to argue.

'There was another lovely incident,' says Smith, 'when Des was covering a rained-off Wimbledon – tennis not football. He had to read out some football results or something when suddenly this jaunty piano music struck up from nowhere. He was a bit taken aback, but quick as a flash he said, "You must excuse me, but it's hard to read these and play the piano at the same time."

'This really amused me, because I reckon you could sort of imagine him playing the piano in the corner of a hotel bar. Yeah, he definitely has that lounge-lizard thing. You can imagine him in the corner of the bar saying, "My dear, would you like to come to my room," pulling on a silk dressing gown and opening champagne. You get the impression that Des would be pretty good in bed.'

Certainly a bemused Smith was able to observe at close quarters the effect Des has on what he himself likes to call 'the ladies' at the wrap party for *My Summer with Des*. He says:

'At the end of show party there were girls I know – women

in their thirties actually – people in high profile positions, who were so thrilled to meet Des. They could hardly contain their excitement.

'I don't imagine they want a night of sordid sex with Des, more they would like him to squire them in his tuxedo to a dinner dance.

'He's got a beautiful voice and there's an Irish quality about him and the way he rolls over his words. It's a bit like that Wogan sort of thing – an easy charm – that comfort with words and people. I think it's a bit of a mystery to him, too.'

After the huge success of *My Summer with Des*, television bosses were keen for Smith to create other vehicles for the laconic presenter but he says:

'I was asked to write a lot of other stuff but I didn't want to end up as some sort of double act with Des.

'I think he had reached the point where the exposure was just enough, too. He seemed to like the play and I think he recognized that it was a nice little push in his career. But it got to the point where it was getting a little too much. If it had gone any further there would have been a backlash but then Des just retreated a little bit back from the limelight.'

The play was broadcast just before the World Cup in France in 1998. And, as ever, Smith was glued to the edge of his seat for the big games – and for Des's immaculate hosting of the BBC coverage. 'He did a superb job in the World Cup,' says Smith. 'There was an added bonus to watching it if Des was presenting.'

England soccer coach Glenn Hoddle famously promised that his team would be the best prepared England side ever to take part in a major championships. The BBC, too, did a thorough job to make sure their 'team' would be fully prepared. In the commentary positions there would be Barry Davies and John

Motson, ably assisted by Ray Stubbs, Tony Gubba and Jon Champion.

In the studio with Des there were his regular sidekicks, Alan Hansen and Jimmy Hill, together with Martin O'Neill, the lively, darting Ulsterman and manager of Leicester City who commands the respect of his Premiership peers, and Frenchman David Ginola, the pin-up idol of Tottenham fans and several million schoolgirls who adore his dark good looks and tumbling mane of thick hair.

Add to that the skills of Gary Lineker, Des's regular stand-in on *Match of the Day*, together with the expertise of Trevor Brooking, Mark Lawrenson and the irascible Ally McCoist and you had to say, the Beeb had a pretty strong hand. Des, who is never happier than when he's 'up against ITV and giving them a smack' had certainly compiled an impressive squad. But presiding over the talented ensemble sometimes required Des to combine the judgment of Solomon with the discipline of an affectionate headmaster to keep 'his boys' in line and on form. The sparks often flew – particularly between Hansen and Hill – and perhaps it was just as well that the flamboyant Newcastle manager Ruud Gullit transferred to ITV before the finals began. His clashes with Hansen on the *Match of the Day* panel had been getting increasingly spicy.

The BBC's headquarters throughout the World Cup was laid out over an entire floor of the RAC Club in Paris – a spot so good, the Germans tried to nick it – and the BBC engineers even brought Paris to a standstill while they constructed an entire outside broadcast unit on the roof of the building.

England's first game of the tournament came on Monday 15 June. They were to take on Tunisia in a group game in Marseilles but there was concern over the dramas in the French city port where English fans had been caught up, once again, in violent clashes.

Des had prepared his script for the big game – typical Lynam stuff – robust, down-to-earth and sparky: 'Tunisia gave Wales a four-nil tonking recently and they could cause big trouble for England here today . . .'

But he was more concerned about his opening remarks: 'So,

you're there then? Shouldn't you lot be at work? Listen, I don't care if you don't care. I'm with you. How could you miss this?' It was a classic Lynam arm-around-the-shoulders, come-and-watch-the-game-with-me intro, but he sought advice from the programme editor Niall Sloane. 'I'm worried about the tone of this, Niall,' he questioned. 'Given the violence in Marseilles, do you think this is too light?' Des is a perfectionist and though everything he says on camera sounds as though it comes off the top of his head, it's mainly scripted hours beforehand. With Des agonizing over every word.

'Nah, Des,' replied Sloane. 'People are going to be tuning in all excited for the match ahead. You can talk about the violence after the chat with Stubbsy (commentator Ray Stubbs) at the ground.'

Satisfied, Des headed off to join the others, but he was also still anxious about a little incident a couple of days earlier when he actually grabbed Alan Hansen's shirt in front of camera to illustrate a point about shirt-tugging on the pitch. He was concerned that the incident made him look a little foolish.

'Can somebody dig out the bit of tape where Hansen and I had the row yesterday,' he asked. Everyone told him to forget about it, but Des phoned Rose, his partner of fifteen years, and asked her, 'Did you see that one, darling? How did it look to you?' Des wants to make sure he's aware of every mistake, no matter how small, so that he never makes the same error again.

A 2–0 victory for Glen Hoddle's team, with goals from captain Alan Shearer and Manchester United's Paul Scholes got the England team, and the BBC squad, on their way in fine style and there was no one more relieved than Des when Shearer slotted the ball home. It's an aspect of Des that the fans at home never get to see. He really *is* into the game – not just out of professional interest, he's a real fan, too.

Martin O'Neill is one of Des's biggest fans. He says:

'He is fantastic, no doubt about it. There is obviously a real natural charm there and I know it's a cliché, but the camera loves him. When people tune in to him they think everything's all right with the world because there's the voice, the look, that knowing little wink he gives, which makes people think: hang on a minute, it's a nice place to be, the world, you know.

'There's almost a reassurance about him, sort of: Hey, listen, we'll be all right, everything will be OK. If he does have to work at it, he does it magnificently to make it look as natural as possible, but I think he's at a stage where he's not having to work at an image.'

Staying at the plush Hotel du Louvre, the panel had the perfect place to refresh their souls and repair their team spirit whenever things went wrong – which they did in dramatic fashion during England's second game. England were caught napping by the sharpshooters of Romania and a last gasp goal from Chelsea player Dan Petrescu, beating his club team-mate Graham Le Saux, the England full back, gave Romania a 2–1 victory. It was a hard defeat to swallow, because Liverpool teenager Michael Owen looked to have saved England's blushes by grabbing an equalizer in the eighty-third minute after coming on as a substitute for Manchester United's Teddy Sheringham.

The hopes of the nation rested on the final group game with Colombia in Lens. The South Americans are so unpredictable, no one was quite sure whether to feel confident or not. Once again, Des and his team could not concentrate purely on the match as trouble flared before the game and once again the English fans featured large. On the pitch, however, Darren Anderton, of Spurs, and David Beckham both scored to give England a comfortable 2–0 victory and a second-stage clash with old rivals Argentina.

It was during the group games that Des astounded his fellow pundits with just how sharp he really could be. The former footballers, whose analysis is part of the great strength of the BBC's coverage of soccer in particular, found that in broadcasting terms they were still apprentices.

Martin O'Neill recalls:

'Most people know about the earpiece which presenters like Des use to be fed information from the producers and editors and all that, and in the World Cup panellists with a fair bit of television experience like Ally McCoist, Alan Hansen and Mark Lawrenson all used an earpiece. I didn't because I couldn't take in the stuff coming down from the studio . . . and be sure that when they came to me, that I would be able to have a conversation while someone else was talking into my ear.

'In one programme there were just fifteen or sixteen seconds left and the dangerous one (Des), he came to me. He must have thought to himself, "Shall I wrap up the programme now or shall I ask Martin another question?" The danger with me is that I will go on and rant and rave a bit for longer than fifteen seconds. Des obviously decided that there was another point that needed making here, but he asked the question in such a way that it required more than a simple yes or no answer, but you knew it had to be short and tight. I wasn't on the earpiece, remember, so I had no idea there were only fifteen seconds to go.

'Ally McCoist was absolutely amazed at Des coming in with a question when they all knew there were just fifteen seconds to go, but I got my answer in and Des still had time to wrap up. Afterwards, McCoist said to Des, "That was absolutely fantastic – especially going to O'Neill there." But Des can do these things by using the inflection in his voice and he's so good at reading you, too.'

Des and colleagues were left kicking their heels for the biggest clash of the tournament so far, England versus Argentina in the first round of the tournament's knockout stages. ITV had the rights to screen the game. And with the country right behind the national team, they capitalized with the biggest audience in British television history. The game was full of unbelievable tension and drama – and saw the making of a hero and a villain. Michael Owen scored, arguably, the best goal of the World Cup but David Beckham was sent off for an unfortunate display of petulant retaliation just two minutes into the second half, which set up a nail-biting classic encounter. The game finished 2–2, even after extra time, but once again, England's hopes were to end in tears in a penalty shoot-out.

First Paul Ince and then David Batty failed to score from the penalty spot to see England's campaign end in heartbreak.

O'Neill adds:

'There was great despondency after the Argentina game but we didn't watch it together because ITV had the coverage and we had no live role that night. Des and the others were disappointed, but they are very professional and just got on with the job. Des takes his sport very seriously and during games he will have an opinion but he will not voice it at the expense of his guests. He allows them to do their work. You feel when he is talking to you that you are not going to be pressurized and even if you say something rather foolish it'll be OK.

'Mind you, if he thought you were getting a little too cocky he can pull you down very nicely, and it would not be noticed by the audience, but you would know.

'I enjoyed working with him and with Hansen and the others. When you are out there with them for a month you do get to know them. We used to eat out in Paris after the programme was over and relax and unwind. Those were excellent evenings.'

One of the strangest sights of the entire World Cup campaign arrived on doormats all over Britain courtesy of the *Sun*, the daily tabloid newspaper with a massive circulation and a reputation for off-the-wall 'exclusives'. Staring out at bleary-eyed Britain from a kneeling position, fists raised in mock celebration, was the familiar moustache and twinkling eyes of Desmond. A banner headline proclaimed, HOD HELP US; while a second headline explained, Des says kneel on the *Sun* and pray for England like me. It was accompanied by a picture of Des as we'd never seen him before – and as we never envisaged we might see him, either.

It was the day of England's crucial clash with Colombia in Lens and some bright spark at the *Sun*'s gloomy headquarters in Wapping had come up with the idea of providing the nation's soccer-holics with a prayer mat on which they could kneel to ask for divine intervention – or at least an Alan Shearer hat-trick – to give England victory. A photograph of the Wembley turf – football's spiritual homeland – was reproduced across the centre pages, complete with the red cross of St George and markings to show exactly how the prayer mat should be used. There was a dotted area marked 'left knee' another one marked 'right knee' and another one marked 'Beer Here'.

The difficulty is, with these things, that to make the joke work, someone with appropriate authority has to 'front them up'. In this instance that had to be Des Lynam – the man the entire nation trusted as the vital link between the action and the home, office or pub.

Des had been 'putting in some training' on the *Sun*'s replica Wembley patch, the newspaper proudly informed us, adding the pun that he had declared it 'a perfect praying surface'. Kneeling on the mat with the Eiffel Tower in the background, Des urged supporters: 'Join me in a prayer for the team and let's put the Colombians out to grass. I'm certainly praying that England will turf out Colombia and go through.'

I vividly remember seeing that picture of Des and, to coin one of his catchphrases, thinking: How did they do that? How did they manage to persuade Des Lynam, of all people, to pose for that? It was so un-Des-like. So uncool. As a stunt it was hilarious and a great coup for the *Sun*. But what on earth possessed Des to go for it? A sense of wonderment echoed throughout the BBC and even Des's inner circle of friends.

A couple of days earlier we had been treated to the spectacle of Des peering out from underneath a plastic *Sun* World Cup bowler hat, sporting a Churchillian finger gesture, and a headline which cried, A DAY OF DES-TINY. In the BBC team's pre-match build-up in their improvised studios at the RAC Club in Paris, Des passed off the episode with a jokey: 'Christ, I look a bit pissed there.' But the underlying reason he agreed to help out with the two stunts clearly baffled his colleagues.

The answer was simple – heartachingly simple for Des. He was made an offer he felt he simply could not refuse. And it had little to do with the £1000 for charity the newspaper was happy to cough up.

For some time, the *Sun* had been pursuing a story that Des Lynam was having an affair with a neighbour – an attractive divorcée. They had evidence of this 'affair' nine months before the World Cup, but in the inner sanctum of *Sun* editor Stuart Higgins's offices, it was decided that, although the story was interesting to the public, it wasn't a matter of public interest. OK, Des was a high profile public figure, but according to one News International executive the general feeling was:

'Well, it's only once and he's not married anyway.

'Des had denied the affair when we fronted him up about it, but we had pictures of the two of them together, which he did not know. We decided not to go ahead and run the story.

'Anyway, information kept on coming in that Des was still seeing his lady friend, behind his long-term partner's back, and we caught the two of them together again. It was when they all went across to Paris and we caught him out again. But the same problem arose – whether it was a suitable story to tell. He knew that he had been caught out before, because we confronted him with it and he just denied it, saying it wasn't true. We never showed him the pictures we had, though.

'This time – we caught him on a Saturday night I think – and so we confronted him on the Sunday. He pleaded that the story should not be used because it was just before the World Cup and he would be dreadfully embarrassed, which were probably his true feelings.

'There was a general feeling that because of the World Cup, and he was lead presenter and all the rest of it, that you weren't going to get much public sympathy for the story and, of course, he might have resigned which was not what anyone would have wanted. So, again, we didn't run the story.'

What happened next was purely fortuitous for the *Sun*. The prayer-mat idea was brokered in the office and everyone agreed it was a typical piece of mercurial *Sun* thinking – to capture the mood of the moment.

'That idea came up just after we had confronted Des about his affair, but the two were not linked. However, we did take advantage, shall we say, of Des's sudden friendship with us by asking him to do the prayer-mat stunt.

'There wasn't any deal done at all, but we just happened to say we were doing this prayer-mat thing all over Britain – people at bus stops and so on – and will you do it. And he did. I think he just thought "I'd better do this . . ." I think he wanted £1000 to be given to a charity of his choosing and we were only too happy to do so. There was no pressure put on him, although I don't know what went through his mind.

'Everyone at the BBC and everyone else thought it was bloody extraordinary him doing it. All his mates thought it was rather astonishing that he had done it. When the *News of the World* revealed details of his affair some time afterwards – after his lady friend had spoken to them – we hardly touched the story.'

The story of how Des began a relationship with a neighbour, Laura Ewing, which continued into the World Cup, was eventually revealed simultaneously in the *News of the World* and the *Mail on Sunday* late in September, 1998. Des appeared to shrug off the unwanted publicity by saying he had made 'an error of judgment'.

When the tournament was over; when France had picked up the cup following a much-deserved 3–0 victory over Brazil; Des worked out a brilliant way to close down his coverage. With a fabulous montage of the passion and excitement, the highs and the heartbreak of the previous month, he indulged his passion for poetry and set the footage to his own voice-over of Rudyard Kipling's famous poem, 'If'. Skilfully pieced with the most moving images from the tournament, the reading added a certain gravity to the closing of a fantastic event. But that wouldn't be Des. He would never leave us in turmoil, with disturbed thoughts, with anything too heavy. And he didn't. With a match-winning quip to compare with Michael Owen's stunning goal against Argentina, after his recitation Des cracked us up with one of his superbly comic one-liners.

'Mr Kipling,' he intoned, with a raising of a bushy eyebrow. 'He does write exceedingly good poems.'

2

When Irish Eyes are Smiling. . .

Thanks, thanks to thee, my worthy friend,
For the lesson thou hast taught!
Thus at the flaming forge of life
Our fortunes must be wrought;
Thus on its sounding anvil shaped
Each burning deed and thought.
'The Village Blacksmith' Henry Wadsworth Longfellow

There's an almost spellbinding mystique surrounding Des. His unplaceable accent, his unflustered nature and his ready wit and warmth seem familiar yet strangely detached. He's the kind of guy who, if he weren't famous, you would meet once and think, 'I'm sure I know him from somewhere.'

It is the 'somewhere' that provides the key to the real Des Lynam. It's not until you hear that Des is actually Irish – born and raised, at least for his first few years, in Ennis, County Clare – that people suddenly realize: 'Oh, yeah. He does have a touch of the Irish about him. Thought he probably was . . .'

The laid-back temperament, the easy way with words and people are characteristics you can easily associate with the lugubrious, story-telling native of the Emerald Isle, like Terry Wogan for instance, one of Des's old radio pals, or even the amiable Guinness-drinking construction worker who came 'across the water' to make a few quid.

His style, his mannerisms, his catchphrases – 'Tell you what', or 'Don't know about you . . .' – seem to draw you into his confidence, invite you to sit down and put your feet up. He's saying, 'You make yourself comfortable, I'll get the beers in.'

To paraphrase the title of one of Des's later non-sporting television successes, 'How Does He Do That?' The answer lies partly in his Irish background and partly in the traumatic events which shaped his later life.

When the infant Desmond Michael Lynam was born on 17 September 1942, he entered into a world of relative innocence and charm. The Second World War was raging across Europe, but in the meadows and traffic-free streets of Ennis young boys could grow in a materially poor but safe environment. Des's parents, Edward and Gertrude, had moved to England before the war started to look for work, but his mother returned to Ireland when Edward was called up and posted to India to serve in the Army Medical Corps.

She moved into an end-of-terrace house in Francis Street which was the home of Des's grandfather, Patrick 'Pako' Malone, a local sporting hero who represented County Clare at both hurling and Gaelic football. 'He tought me how to fish and I went shooting with him,' says Des, 'He was the father figure really, we were very close.' Next door were his uncle and aunt, Frank and Kitty Malone. Frank was a well-known farrier – the last blacksmith in Ennis – and when little Desmond came along he instantly became the apple of everyone's eye. Reminiscing he recalls: 'I arrived in the middle of the night, a week or two late, and my mother said, "He didn't want to come out. He was happier where he was." I was over 10 lbs at birth and was a real podge as a toddler. They thought I was going to be a bit of a fatty.'

Young Des had grown to a little scamp of three, though, before he set eyes on his father for the first time at the end of the war. 'It must have been tricky for him at first,' says the thoughtful Des, 'coming home and trying to get my affection. I was three years old and I thought, "Who is this strange guy coming to pick me up?" '

The house stands opposite St Mary's Franciscan Church on what is the oldest road in the town, linking, as it did, the Franciscan Abbey at Ennis with Clonroad Castle. Today, it is a hairdresser's shop and few of the residents nearby are aware that a little boy who once played hurling and football up and down the street is now one of the most famous faces in British sports broadcasting.

Des returns to the area from time to time. His favourite golf course is half an hour's drive away from Ennis at Lahinch. But although the town promotes itself as the technology centre of West Ireland, with an ever-present strapline of 'Information Age Town' seemingly grafted onto the name Ennis, he would still raise a wry smile at some of the endearing characteristics and old-fashioned charm which survive – like a beauty parlour called Wrinkles or the Snow White launderette. Having written a couple of earnest verses for a volume of poetry, he might even find time for a drink in the Poets' Corner bar at the town's Old Ground Hotel.

Ennis printer Paddy Brennan, who is three years younger than Des, takes a trek down memory lane and remembers:

'It was a good time to be a child. There were hardly any motor cars around at that time and one game we all played was just sitting by the side of the road watching the few cars that would come along and counting them. At school we'd boast about who had seen the most.

'At nights there would be card games and storytelling. There was no television in those days but there were some very good travelling storytellers. They would call at your house and for the price of a meal and a bed for the night they would regale you with the most fantastic and wonderfully told stories. They were spellbinding. All of this would have been part and parcel of Des's everyday life.

'The children would play all sorts of athletics and games of hurling and football in the Fairgreen and then there were seasonal pastimes like conkers, burning "Blackie Tops", picking nuts, sloes, blackberries, crab apples and "rawking" known orchards for apples in the autumn.

'The winter was a time for storytelling, as Father would often read the comic strips from the newspaper for us at night after we said the rosary. Whenever there was frost, we spent many hours skating on ice in Hogan's field or on the concrete paths down from the Club Bridge.

'In moments of mischief we sometimes tied a number of the door knockers together and from across the road where we hid, a long piece of cord or thread would be used to knock on all the doors together. It was very funny to see four or five people come to their front doors together to answer the call.

'Spring was taken up with racing hoops – the wheel of a bike minus the spokes. The elite of the town had tyres around their hoops. Marbles were very popular and for those who couldn't afford marbles, the games would be played with corks.

'Catching "torniebacks" – fish fry – was one of our great passions. We brought them home in jam jars and tried to keep them alive for as long as possible. This would be down at a little stream in Corrovorrin which we called Andy Burke's Harbour. Many mothers brought their families to that little stream for picnics. The ladies exchanged local gossip while the children swam, bathed or caught torniebacks in the stream. In many cases these breaks constituted the summer holidays as the families could not afford to go to Lahinch or the seaside.

'Des would also remember the Corpus Christi processions held every year on 15 August. They always left from the friary opposite Des's house and everyone in the town took part in it. The procession travelled all around the town before an outdoor service in the local market.'

The Roman Catholic church played a large part in every family's life – as it still does today – and the Malones, with young Desmond and Mrs Lynam in residence, were no exception. Schooling was conducted by the nuns at the Holy Family School for the young ones and the stern Christian Brothers made sure the older boys and girls took their education seriously.

It's a period of his life that Des remembers well, despite his tender years. Asked once if he was too young to have any memories of Ireland he replied, slipping easily into a rich Irish brogue: 'God, no. You see, when you've got Irish parents they're always going home for the holidays. We were in Ireland every summer, so I felt as if I was still there.'

Today in Ennis, you can meet fabulous characters who could show even our Des a thing or two about storytelling. Local historian Sean Spellissy revels in tales of the town's warlike ancestors, the O'Briens, descendants of the famed Irish king Brian Boru, who fought the Anglo-Norman invaders of Munster in the late twelfth century; and later of the MacNamaras who fought against Oliver Cromwell.

By the late nineteenth century, Ennis had become an important town in the west of Ireland, famous for its campaigns on electioneering rights, for its three bridges over the River Fergus and its superb salmon fishing. Heroes of modern Irish culture like Charles Stewart Parnell, Daniel O'Connell and Edward de Valera were regular visitors. But this description of the town by Bernard Becker, described as a 'special commissioner of the *Daily News*', who visited Ennis in 1880, is not to be missed.

Arriving at half-past eight one morning, with hardly a soul stirring, Becker recorded:

> 'In the main street I observed six grog-shops, side by side, actually shoulder to shoulder, cheek by jowl. Another street appeared to be all grog-shops but for the ominous exception of an undertaker.
>
> 'About nine o'clock a few people came out of chapel and shortly afterwards the butchers' shops gave signs of life, one opening on each side of the main street, and blinking like a bloodshot eye upon the slumbering groceries and groggeries, drapery stores and general drowsiness.'

The town still boasts a prolific selection of pubs and a sleepy air during what city folk might deem 'rush hour'.

A few years earlier, the *Limerick Chronicle*, describing pleas at an insolvency debtors' court in Limerick City, recorded: 'It is quite true, my lord, that he got into debt in Ennis. It is a well known fact that perhaps a more immoral town, or a place more calculated to lead a young man astray, is not to be found in Ireland.'

Welcome to laid-back Lynam's home town.

To meet the modern-day residents of Ennis, to talk about their reminiscences, and to read about their history from the 'Great Hunger' of the mid nineteenth century when the potato famine ravaged the land, through to the great political reformers and orators who came from the area, is to get some measure of Des's heritage. Maybe, perhaps, some insight into the complexity of his personality. His early days were blissfully carefree yet he has inherited a steely toughness – maybe stubbornness – which many can testify has manifested itself in the way in which he single-mindedly pursued his ambitions in later years.

The fact that his father was away at war during his earliest years is unlikely to have had much impact on how Des developed – except, perhaps, to form a stronger attachment to his mother. If one parent is absent, it simply means there's a less diluted parenthood and in Des's case this meant his mother caring for all his needs. In addition, if he needed a strong male figure, he need look no further than his grandfather, whom he adored.

Des, though, left this rural idyll when he was just six years old. With the war over and Des's father returned from India, the family tried once again to make a new start in England. They took the boat and moved to Brighton where Lynam senior found employment as a mental health officer and Gertrude subsequently became a nurse. Life for the hard-working couple was not without even greater hardship than being parted for years by the war, though.

Gertrude gave birth to a sister for Desmond, Anne, but the family suffered a terrible trauma when Anne died in infancy from meningitis. They almost lost Des, too, when the boy suffered a septic appendix, complicated by the onset of measles.

It was a traumatic period from which even the innocence of childhood couldn't shield Des. Des is quite wistful about the fact that he had a sister; that she didn't survive to grow up with him is still clearly quite painful. He feels that a sibling, particularly a sister, would have had an important bearing on his life. Maybe even changed the way things have turned out.

When it comes to the personal stuff, Des notoriously has one of the tightest defences in broadcasting's premiership. He gives nothing away at all if he can help it. But during the World Cup in France in 1998, he did relax enough in conversation with one interviewer to reveal: 'At that age, you're shielded from the grief by your own simplicity. It's a great regret she didn't live; my sister would have changed my life. Changed it for the better.'

Of his own brush with death, Des says:

'I was more or less a healthy child, but I caught measles when I was five or six and had appendicitis at the same time and nearly snuffed it. My parents really thought I was a goner and, being Catholics, called the priest.

'I was desperately ill, out of action for some months and pretty debilitated. To the point where I had been in bed so long – first in hospital, then at home – I had to go to a clinic to learn to walk again and do exercises with cotton reels to strengthen my toes.'

He was, in fact, rather luckier than it first appears. The first doctor called to attend him thought it was merely a case of 'acid tummy' and recommended a dose of appropriate medicine. Fortunately, his father, who wasn't happy with the diagnosis, had the strength of mind to call for a second opinion. Remember that in those days – these days, too, in some instances – doctors thought that they were God and any mere mortal questioning their opinion would have been thought of as quite outrageous. Anyway, the second doctor recognized the urgency of the problem immediately and growled, 'The boy has a septic appendix.'

Des was rushed to hospital and emergency surgery saved his life. Quite by chance, the doctor who saved Des's life, Dr John O'Hara, later became a much-respected figure within the

Football Association. He served on several committees and was made a life member.

Those early hard times; the trauma of moving to England and the fact that he lost a sibling are likely to have had a 'steeling' effect on Des's personality, made him tougher. Certainly they have given him the personality to become a more capable adult.

The family lived in a small terraced house and although money was tight, his parents made every effort to ensure that the youngster didn't miss out. There was always enough money for the right sort of gym shoes and schoolwear and, like every boy of that era, a new bike made a memorable impression on him. As he grew up, family outings would include visits to Brighton's Hippodrome Theatre where Des was entranced by stand-up comedians like Max Bygraves and Vic Oliver. All of those comedians used to have a catchphrase, and many years later, Des brought catchphrases to the world of television sport with his jaunty '. . . Tell you what . . .' or 'Don't know about you . . .'

Des recalls the move to Brighton – and the effect he had on the neighbours. He says: 'I had a very broad West of Ireland accent when we arrived in Brighton. When we first moved in our neighbours couldn't understand a word I said.'

Of course, there is no trace of that accent today and people are genuinely surprised the first time they hear that Des is Irish. He insists that he didn't make a conscious effort to erase all traces of his boyhood or dramatically reinvent himself but he does recall one amusing, yet painful, incident which obviously left an impression on him.

'Yes, there was one incident I remember where a teacher said, "Draw a line," and I drew a little creature with four legs and a mane,' says Des. 'I must have been stupid. Got a smack on the back of my hand. I suppose in my subconscious I thought I'd better get rid of this accent.'

The wonderful imagery is classic Lynam.

The move from a small Irish market town to the hurly burly and bustle of Brighton – no doubt combined with the effects of an almost incomprehensible accent – made Des a shy and reserved pupil, first at the local Catholic primary school, and then at the prestigious Varndean Grammar School. In his little red blazer and short grey trousers Des was certainly full of trepidation on his first day at Varndean. The school, founded in 1884, with its atmospheric cloistered corridors, was quite an intimidating place for any boy of eleven tender years.

One former pupil recalls:

'The Headmaster at the time was Eric John Hutchins, a very authoritarian figure, who scared the pants off all new boys like Des and myself. It was a school of traditions and Hutchins himself was only the school's third head in its entire history. He was a man of, how should we say, very singular opinions. I think most pupils had a love-hate relationship with him.

'The school had a good academic record but was also immensely proud of its sporting prowess. Sport was considered very important – cricket, football, hockey, athletics, that sort of thing. I have no recollection of Des being any sort of sporting giant. In fact he is remembered as rather a quiet individual.'

Des's own sporting prowess, it seems, was limited to the odd appearance for the school football team. Although in those formative years he might have been developing a deep affection for sport, he remained pretty much on the sidelines as far as participating was concerned.

He was a tall, rather thin, gangling sort of lad and almost painfully shy.

It's hard to imagine, these days, that Des Lynam was ever reticent about speaking up for himself, but the paradox of someone shy choosing a career which calls for performing in public and addressing audiences which run into millions is not lost on him. He recalls being asked to read out loud in class as a fourteen-year-old, saying: 'They would have to pull it out of me. I had lots of opinions but I didn't want to draw attention to myself by expressing them. There's still a reluctance to stand up and say a few words off the top of my head. When I'm asked to do it I am fine but feel really nervous.'

One thing which was missing from Varndean Grammar School was girls. The red-brick grammar was a boys-only school sitting on a hillside overlooking Brighton and the sea. The girls' school was close by, in full view across the playing fields. Some might say that Des's notorious eye 'for the ladies' has its roots in the fact that there were precious few around in those anxious days of transition from boy to youth to man.

He was certainly aware enough of 'the ladies' – as he himself always refers to the fair sex – by the age of fifteen to be mortified when, during one of his outings with the school football team, an opponent kicked him in the face, causing one of his front teeth to fall out. 'I was so vain, I thought it was the end of the world,' he says.

Still, without the permanent distraction of *cherchez la femme* along the school corridors, Des proved to be a good student. He moved onwards and upwards into the sixth form, delighted to exchange the schoolboy's red blazer for a more sophisticated navy blue jacket which the older boys were allowed to wear. Even in those days Des had sartorial taste. He passed with flying colours his A levels in English, French and Art and could quite easily have gone on to university but chose not to. Today it's a missed opportunity he bitterly regrets.

However, he insists, he didn't want to be a financial burden on his parents any longer and, instead, went to Brighton Business College where he studied for, sat and passed exams for the Chartered Insurance Institute. The bright young hopeful immediately landed a job with Cornhill Insurance and, for the next eight years, the world of sport had almost let this genuine 24-carat talent slip through the net.

To learn that Des Lynam was an insurance salesman is like someone trying to convince you that Alan Shearer really wanted to be a nurse; or that Jimmy Hill's chin isn't really big, it's just a distortion of the camera. It's just hard to take in. But anyone who thinks this could be a source of amusement will get short shrift from Des. To him, any job he does – or has done – is no laughing matter. That's part of his professionalism.

Or, maybe, it's more to do with pride. Ego, even.

If he had stayed in insurance rather than finding his way into television, where would he have been today? 'I think I'd have done well,' he says. 'Probably made more money. I was an inspector – partly sales, partly doing surveys of buildings and all that thing. Technical stuff. Had to train for it. People say, "Oh, he was a door-to-door salesman." Well, I certainly wasn't that. My bit of pride in my past profession comes out there. It was certainly more than that.'

Without a doubt it was more than going 'on the knocker' flogging life policies to bored housewives – although that, somehow, is the image we would all really like to have of Des the salesman. The good people of Sussex would, you feel, be more comprehensively covered than anywhere else in the country if Des had had to work his charm over the threshold of countless suburban vestibules.

He went into insurance in 1960 and was soon made an inspector, calling at farms, factories, shops, offices, garages and other commercial premises throughout East Sussex. A spokesman for Cornhill says:

'He was out on the road, but it was never door-to-door selling. He handled motor, household and general business insurance. He would talk to insurance brokers about Cornhill products and persuade them to place business with us.

'When they did he would go along and survey the premises, asking if they needed extra locks or fire extinguishers and what have you, and looking at the construction of the property concerned. He would be assessing the risk. He started out freelancing sports reports for newspapers and radio while he was with us, but one day he just packed in his job and went off to pursue what we all thought was his hobby. He moved on to something which he considered much more exciting and dynamic.'

Des was popular on his 'beat' which included Brighton and Eastbourne, Hastings, Lewes, Uckfield and Crowborough. But his already highly-preened dress sense did at least once make it difficult for him to perform to his own most particular standards according to Cornhill legend.

Some time after Des left the insurance world, another inspector called at a particularly muddy farmyard in East Sussex to draw up a new insurance schedule. He was armed with Des's original file and was surprised to find several differences between how the farm looked then, and how it appeared in the Lynam report. 'I'm not bloody surprised,' said the farmer. 'The other bloke never got out of the car.'

Apparently it had been a particularly wet day when Des visited and the ever-present mud would have ruined his highly polished brogues and immaculate grey flannels so he made his best guess from the safety of his company car and returned to his carpeted office without half of East Sussex on his shoes.

What there is no doubt about is that Des grew increasingly restless in his job. At first he felt frustrated, then trapped and then finally he almost hated it. He knew that he had a talent for writing and by 1967 he had begun writing freelance articles and then covering soccer for the local radio station.

After a great deal of soul searching, Des decided to pack in the comfortable job and pin his hopes and ambitions on following his 'hobby' as he referred to his early broadcasting adventures. His great rock of support – and the only person in his life who urged him to take that giant leap of faith – was his wife Susan.

Des met Susan when he was still at Varndean Grammar. She was a pupil at the girls' school and the couple were introduced at a school dance. 'He was a friend of a friend,' recalls Susan. 'He was tall and very good looking, although he was a little skinny and very, very shy. I fell in love with his voice the moment I heard him speak, though.'

This was the beginning of Des's first great love affair but one which, ultimately, was doomed. The couple fell deeply in love and eventually married only for the union to end in bitter tears.

For years he has had to live with the 'Dishy Des' tag and a reputation as a 'ladies' man' with a roving eye. When you learn that his marriage broke up and Des got divorced you might well think, 'Oh, it was probably Des's fault. He probably flirted with disaster once too often . . .'

Not so. The harsh truth is that Susan, lonely as Des chased his career prospects, cheated on him with another man. It was a bitter blow that Des may not yet have fully got over. It certainly helps to explain his reluctance to accept commitment and his near pathological desire for privacy.

Susan, now a glamorous fifty-something blonde who still lives in Brighton, sighs: 'Our marriage lasted eight years, but in the end we got divorced and I was the guilty party. I found somebody else. Des was very hurt. It's not something we have ever been able to talk much about, though we are good friends.

'Des is, and always has been, such a good friend to me.'

The cracks began to appear in their relationship after Des got his job on BBC radio in London. He travelled up to Broadcasting House every day from Brighton and the long hours of work and travelling put a strain on the marriage that is common to the many thousands who endure the daily routine of commuting.

Des also had to 'show his face' in the BBC bar and have the occasional drink with colleagues and broadcasting bosses. It's all part and parcel of the daily lifestyle and essential networking if you are keen to get on in your career when you work in the media.

Meanwhile Susan was stuck at home in Brighton, her sense of loneliness exacerbated by the fact that she was caring for their young son, Patrick, who was only a baby. Susan has amazingly pretty blue eyes, neat blonde hair and keeps herself in trim with regular tennis matches. She is very attractive and Des was reckoned to have found himself quite a catch.

She says: 'I just felt lonely. I was looking after a young child and Des was away from home putting in long hours at the BBC. Eventually I met a man at a party and began an affair. When Des found out about the affair he hit the roof. I regretted it, but it was all too late.'

Des was devastated. As a Catholic, divorce would have been a traumatic choice to make but he was so angry and hurt that there was to be no rescuing of his marriage. He also adored his son Patrick but he was stunned by Susan's betrayal. Theirs was not a marriage accustomed to stormy weather. In general they rarely fell out and any amount of ill-feeling was short-lived.

'We did sort of think about trying to get back together again,' says Susan wistfully,

'but I was scared that it might not work and I did not want Patrick to get used to a situation only for us to part again. We talked of going on a holiday together but I didn't want to risk it really.

'The relationship I entered into was a disaster. It was bad news. The man involved appeared to be the type who paid you a lot of attention but he was a very jealous-natured person. It lasted for six years and then we split up. He is still the same. People don't change.'

Susan was the daughter of a prominent Brighton undertaker Stanley Skinner and his wife and they lived in a large and comfortable house on the outskirts of the town. The family had their own tennis court and Des used to love playing in the friendly tennis matches the Skinners frequently organized. Susan says:

'We met at a school dance, though it wasn't at his school. He was very entertaining. I fell in love with his voice. He didn't really have an accent by that time but his "s's" were very Irish – the way he rolled them over.

'Des was a friend of a friend. I was very shy but he had a shy personality too. To get confidence he made people laugh. We went out together for six years before we got married.

'He was quite a romantic and he used to sing to me – Nat King Cole songs, I seem to remember. He had a good voice. He also used to write poetry – not for me, it was just one of his interests. He wrote quite a lot when his mother died. He was very close to her and her death had a big effect on him.'

They had been together for six years when Susan finally dug her heels in and gave Des an ultimatum: marry me or leave me alone. Even then, Des was in no hurry to make a commitment.

Susan says: 'I don't remember him proposing to me. I think it was a threat from me, either we get married or we split up. I guess you could say I dragged him to the altar.'

They married at St Mary's Church in the Preston Park district of Brighton on 2 October 1965. Desmond, who was then an insurance company inspector, was twenty-three and his bride, Susan Eleanor Skinner was a twenty-one-year-old beautician. Des lived in Elm Road, half a mile back from the sea, in a very ordinary terraced house opposite the Wellington public house. These days the area is slightly run-down and popular with students. Many of the houses have been converted into flats and bedsits. Susan's family came from a more elegant part of town.

St Mary's, where the ceremony was conducted, is an impressive stone-built Roman Catholic church built in 1910, with a spectacular tower and picturesque stained-glass windows.

As befitted the daughter of a prominent local businessman, the wedding was a grand affair with Des and the other chief wedding guests wearing morning suits. The wedding took place on a beautiful sunny day in the midst of a prolonged hot spell and the ceremony was conducted by Father J.W. Wilson and witnessed by registrar P.V. Fairey.

'Our wedding day was lovely,' recalls Susan.

'It was gloriously hot and we had a lot of people over from Ireland. I thought the world of Des's family. His mum and dad were wonderful people and his relatives from Ennis were marvellous. We used to visit them and I always thoroughly enjoyed myself.

'Des was very handsome. He had that lean and hungry look about him. I always thought he looked like the actor Montgomery Clift.'

The happy couple spent their honeymoon night in Arundel, near the famous castle, before setting off for a honeymoon on the Isle of Wight. 'I do remember the hotel on the Isle of Wight,' laughs Susan. 'This woman thought that we would always be together, Des and I, because the hotel was full of wedding couples but we were the only couple who spoke to each other. The rest were just gazing into each other's eyes.'

Unfortunately the hotelier had about as much foresight as a crystal-ball gazer on Brighton pier.

A couple of years later Des was getting desperately fed up of life in the insurance world. His freelance articles and his sporting commentaries for Radio Brighton had opened Des's eyes to a much more exciting world – one for which he knew he had the talent and ability. He also had the hunger to succeed. Though it was a massive step to leave a secure and well-paid job for an uncertain future in the media, it was a move he had to make.

Susan recalls:

'He didn't just come home one day and say he was leaving Cornhill, we discussed it many times. He had been doing a lot of work freelancing and I was the only one who encouraged him. His parents were against the idea.

'He was so unhappy in his job, I said you have got to do it. If you fail it doesn't matter but at least you will have tried. I got myself a different job, at the library, one which paid a little better. But, of course, then I found out I was pregnant. The timing was not brilliant to say the least.'

The couple were thrilled at the prospect of their first child and when Susan finally went into labour Des accompanied her to the maternity unit at Brighton hospital. He was anxious to support his young wife, but like many men in his situation he was more than a little concerned about being a part of the 'big event'. There's a nice birth announcement I once spotted in a local paper which read: 'Baby flawless, mother breathless, father legless.'

Des was in the latter category – though not through drink. He confesses:

'When Patrick was born it was such a thrill. His mother was unwell for a while after the birth. Felt a bit groggy myself.

'It was terribly embarrassing. There I was all wrapped up in gown, mask, gloves and hat. But I wasn't actually there for his arrival because I turned green. Had to be taken out.

'Didn't want to be there in the first place, to tell you the truth. But I felt morally obliged.'

It was shortly after the new arrival in the Lynam household that Des became busier and busier and more and more in demand as a broadcaster. Susan says: 'Des made the move to radio and he was obviously very good. He only worked for Radio Brighton for a short while then he got a job with the BBC in London on Radio Two.'

Unfortunately, that was also the start of their problems.

'Des was putting so much effort into his job that I was feeling quite lonely,' says Susan.

'Just having had a child it was quite difficult. We didn't really think about moving up to London. We were still quite young and, well, we just didn't think of moving. If we had moved up to London we might still have been together.

'When Des was at home he was really good company. He would always make you laugh. If he upset me, he was always keen to make it up. He didn't like it if you cried or anything. He's not the type to deliberately hurt you.'

Day-to-day family life was happy enough. The couple had no money worries and family holidays usually consisted of trips to Ireland and holidays afloat. 'One of our best holidays was spent sailing in Scotland,' says Susan. 'It rained every day, but it didn't seem to matter. On another holiday we went to the Norfolk Broads and I remember Des bumping us into another boat when he was driving. This other chap wasn't very happy, but I was in hysterics.'

Susan also recalls that, although Des was a fabulous husband and father, he was practically useless around the house. 'He was no good at DIY,' she laughs.

'I used to do it all. I got quite good at it. I wouldn't say that he was lazy around the house – though my mother probably would.

'I remember him trying to take a fireplace out once but he didn't have a clue. An electrician came round and saw him doing this very badly and he said, "You don't want to do it like that . . ." He started to show Des what to do and ended up taking the whole fireplace out for us.'

Back at Broadcasting House, Des loved working in radio but his budding talent had been quickly spotted by eagle-eyed editors in television sport. They courted him with impressive offers and eventually he gave in. But it was not a decision he took lightly. Susan says:

'He took ages going to TV. He loved radio and for a long time he just didn't want to go to television. I think he was worried about the backstabbing which goes on in television. The first time we saw him on screen was fantastic. Patrick was only two and he went up to the television and said, "Daddeee . . ."

'Even now it's lovely seeing him on screen. But then, of course, there were the pressures on our marriage. I think that Des believes the long hours of his job were the cause of our marriage failure. It was such a shame. I was so young – it would be late at night before Des usually got home.

'I know what it was like. You have to get your face known in those early days.

'I think it was the timing that broke us up. If I had had Patrick later, when he was established in his job, when I had got used to the hours, when he wasn't still trying to make an impression . . .

'After we split up, Des used to bring his girlfriends to my house and leave them with me while he took Patrick off. It's quite funny really. We are more like brother and sister really, with deeper feelings. I think he thinks I'm a bit mad. He would say to Patrick, "What crazy thing is your mother up to now?" '

Susan stayed in Brighton and has always kept in touch with Des. They both adore their son, Patrick, who decided not to follow his father into television – although he is connected to the industry, working for the audience research group BARB. Susan, who these days bears a remarkable resemblance to Des's current partner, Rose Diamond, with whom he has shared his life for fifteen years, still clearly cares deeply for Des but she adds:

'I can't have any regrets, can I, otherwise I wouldn't be able to go on. I'm not in a relationship – I think I'm doomed. Des is a hard act to follow.

'I'm not jealous of Des or his lifestyle. In fact we get on quite well. I do sometimes think of what might have been. My life would have been totally different. I have met Rose and she's a lovely lady. I'm probably more confrontational than Rose, I would get my back up at some of the things Des does. Rose is very good to him.

'He has always been a flirt, but then, so am I. We were both flirts.

'Patrick is so like his dad. He is more like his grandfather actually, in personality. He is very laid back. Des's father was a lovely man. We were very close to him. We hadn't long been married when his mum died. We had just bought a home. It was a terrible time. He was very close to his mum. He was close to his dad, too, but in a different way. We used to call him "Pops" and he was a real character. They were very much in love and I remember he used to pick her up and carry her around.

'If his mother was alive I don't think we would have split up. She was a strong lady. She would have made me see sense. I was a bit selfish, looking back.'

Des is still anguished that his parents never lived to see his phenomenal success. His mother died of a brain haemorrhage at the age of fifty-four which devastated the entire family. His father Edward moved in with Des and Susan for a time, but he, too, died prematurely through illness seven years later. He suffered from bowel cancer and Des later helped to make a public information film about the terrible disease, though he was barely able to choke back the emotion he felt while filming it.

In an article for the *Daily Telegraph* during the World Cup, interviewer Alison Pearson describes Des's eyes filling with tears at the painful memories and says: 'He (Des) says he can hear them exclaiming, Well, will you look at our Des! "It would have been a thrill for them. And also I'd have been able to do things for them. Make their quality of life better. Say, look, here's a couple of air tickets. But what can you do? What can you do." '

He talked more about his parents while promoting his album of poetry readings, *Time To Stand and Stare,* just before Christmas in 1998. He told the *Sunday Telegraph* magazine that his mother's collapse was 'a sudden thing. The artery just burst. She didn't die straight away. Hung on for a month. My father and I went to see her every day and we kept telling each other that she was looking better. We were desperate to believe it. Clinging to it. I thought, "I shall never worry about anything ever again because nothing can be as bad as this." I guess that feeling lasted two weeks. Mundane things come flooding back.'

About his father, Des says: 'We thought it was going to be a pretty straightforward operation. I wasn't told enough. One of my biggest regrets is that I didn't get the surgeon up against a wall to tell me everything. I felt alone in the world after Dad died because I was recently divorced and had no siblings.

'Well, I had a sister, but she died in infancy from meningitis.'

Susan agrees that the trauma of losing his parents is still painful for Des but he has, like us all, had to get on with life. 'These days I'm happy for Des,' she says. 'When you've loved a person you can be happy for them even though things haven't worked out for you. I'm basically quite a happy person. I'd like to have a man in my life, but he's a hard act to follow. We stayed in regular contact – not just over Patrick – but he doesn't call as much now.'

After the breakdown of his marriage, Des moved to a flat in Patcham village just outside Brighton, and divided his time between there and a flat in Marylebone, London, convenient for the BBC studios. He loves Brighton and remained anxious to spend as much time as he possibly could there.

Although it took him a long time to get over the disappointment and pain of his failed marriage, Des picked up the threads of his bachelor life and was a frequent visitor to Brighton's Kings Club and Theatre Royal. An ardent supporter of Brighton and Hove Albion, he would take Patrick along to games as often as he possibly could – his duties with *Grandstand* permitting – and his greatest pleasure was having the youngster over to stay at his flat.

These days he still divides his time between London and the south coast but his two homes are somewhat more luxurious. In Chiswick, he lives in a magnificent riverside home, with his partner Rose Diamond and their dog Daisy, a West Highland terrier.

On the south coast, however, he has moved a few miles away from cosmopolitan Brighton to find the kind of peace and solitude which would inevitably be denied him in his home town. He hates being recognized in the street and the constant calls of 'Oi, Des' or, 'Tell you what' from building site labourers or other misguided fans. Or even, on one occasion when he was presenting *How Do They Do That* on television, from a taxi driver who called out: 'Oi, Des . . . How do they wossname . . . ?' It's a part of fame he has never quite got used to.

A few years ago he bought a delightful detached home on a quiet, private estate near the village of East Preston. Backing on to a pretty stretch of shingle beach, the home is the perfect hideaway. Des and Rose love it there so much they spend as much time there as possible away from the media frenzy of London life. It boasts four bedrooms and three bathrooms, a snooker room, lounge, dining room, conservatory, office space and pretty patio. The house is extremely stylish, as you might expect, but Des and Rose steadfastly resist the kind of over-the-top ostentation that afflicts those with more money than sense. One local comments: 'They are such a lovely couple. They want peace and quiet and they have found the perfect spot for it. No one who lives there would be the slightest bit interested or concerned about Des's celebrity status.

'The house has been beautifully renovated and they have resisted the temptation to go too far. It would appear they have chosen sensible quality over outrageous luxury.'

Sounds like Des. To a tee!

3

Radio Days . . . and Rainy Saturdays

He either fears his fate too much,
Or his deserts are small,
That puts it not unto the touch
To win or lose it all.
'My Dear and Only Love', James Graham,
Marquess of Montrose, 1612–50

There was, as usual, a stiff breeze blowing across the promenade at Brighton causing Des Lynam's raincoat to flap about like a seagull's wings. He pulled the collar up round his ears and ducked his head down into his chest. The wind seemed colder than usual. He was nervous.

Not given to attacks of the collywobbles, sudden panics or even fear of his superiors in the insurance world, Des was surprised at how much he really, really wanted to be taken on by the fledgling radio station which had recently advertised for enterprising individuals to staff their operation. Approaching the tiny studios at the impressive Royal Pavilion in Brighton, his mouth was dry and he wondered – just for a moment – if things really were all that bad in the familiar world of insurance where he was currently making a good living.

Perhaps it was more a fear of the unexpected. He knew that he had a talent for writing, but broadcasting . . . well, that could be the start of something big. He allowed himself a little daydream before ducking through the doors for the interview which was to change his suburban life.

Like the sporting heroes he brings into millions of homes through television today – the Alan Shearers of football, the Tim Henmans of tennis or the Frank Brunos of boxing – Des didn't start at the top of his trade. Not for him the soccer boot-room or a back-street gymnasium, but he served a useful and somewhat obscure 'apprenticeship' as a broadcaster on Radio Brighton. They were fun-filled, fly-by-the-seat-of-your-pants days where every fresh broadcast brought a new lesson or problem.

The BBC was hardly 'steam radio' by the mid 1960s but the creation of dozens of local radio stations around the country did revive that pioneering spirit of early broadcasting where money was tight, listeners were few and problems were there to be tackled head on.

Stanley Allen, one of Des's first broadcasting colleagues, was a solicitor when he spotted an advertisement in the local *Brighton Evening Argus* newspaper looking for bright young things with an interest in radio. Just like Des, he was intrigued and was eventually invited for an audition at the Royal Pavilion studios.

He recalls:

'Des and I were part of the original Radio Brighton sports team. He was jolly good. It was a very nice setup but Radio Brighton was run on a shoestring and most of the contributors were amateurs like myself. I did cricket and Des did football and boxing.

'When local radio started in the 1960s all the stations were told to raise their own finances and to rely on local populists to do a lot of work for them. In other words we were cheap labour. There was an advert in the *Argus* for people who thought they could do something. I went along for an audition, like we all did.

'I actually wanted to do quizzes and they asked if there was anything else I wanted to do. I said cricket commentating so they said OK, do a blind commentary on one over.

That was it, I was in. Des was the same, except he wanted to do football and boxing.

'None of us particularly had any newspaper connections or qualifications. I was a solicitor and Des was an insurance agent and so on and so forth. It was hilarious in a way and we enjoyed ourselves enormously. We always went into the pub after we had done a broadcast. There was a team of about six or seven of us.

'Des was a lovely character, a smooth operator and he obviously had a good broadcasting voice. He was an extrovert, a great chap, easy going and friendly.'

At this time, Des lived in Queen's Park Road, Brighton, and was working full time as an insurance agent for Cornhill. But like his new radio colleagues he obviously felt something was missing in his life. For some that gap is filled by amateur dramatics or, maybe, going fishing. For Des and those other local radio pioneers, it was the electric thrill of chasing down the local sporting news and pinging it out over the airwaves to a small but appreciative audience.

'We all met when the station opened,' recalls Stanley. 'We had a professional producer who was in charge of the sports team and we used to get together on a Monday night to do a sports programme and, of course, every Saturday. It worked incredibly well. I thought we were quite good. Looking back now we were probably awful, but we thought we were good at the time.'

Those fun amateur days for Des were a far cry from life at the heart of one of the most sophisticated broadcasting setups in the world. John Henty, who was the sports producer on Radio Brighton and, therefore, Des's first broadcasting boss recalls how he had a budget of just £15 to bring out a programme.

Just one edition of *Match of the Day* costs the BBC more in the region of £600,000, mainly, of course, due to the hefty fees paid to the Premier League for the rights to screen games.

Something else was incredibly different, though, too. The glossy *Match of the Day* studio, and those at ITV, set off the professional tone and tenor of Des and his team, but in his early days at Radio Brighton Des had to be content with broadcasting from a garden shed, crudely perched at the back of the terraces at Brighton and Hove Albion's Goldstone ground. The sports team had to build it themselves and Des may even have had to lend a hand to creosote the makeshift studio.

John Henty says:

'Desmond Lynam honed his skills in that garden shed. We would broadcast live from the Goldstone ground, but we didn't have a permanent position. I'll never forget our first outside broadcast from the ground and the reason we had to build the shed – it was Albion versus Wolverhampton Wanderers in some minor cup competition. We turned up and the Press box was full, so we sat in some seats only to be told by some regulars, "They're our seats." We moved to some more seats, but again the regular occupants arrived and we ended up ducking down in the aisle and trying to cover the game from there.

'Unfortunately, while we were being moved about, Wolves scored. There was a deathly hush from the mainly home fans, so we didn't realize a goal had been scored and we broadcast the whole of the first half under the mistaken impression that it was nil apiece. It was only when a policeman who was outside the ground phoned the radio station to tell them what a cock-up we were making, that we found out. Fortunately for Des, he wasn't on that broadcast, but it was the incident that spurred us into getting the garden shed.

'We built it up ourselves. I can't remember if Des had to creosote it or not, but it was certainly rudimentary. We had to move the shed around to various parts of the Goldstone ground as the club decided they needed this space or that space. But it's where both Des and Peter Brackley learnt their trade. I clearly remember him in that shed on the back of the terraces.'

Something else Des will remember vividly as he ruminates on the mega-bucks offers which regularly come his way, is the fact that he only got paid £2 for his early sporting stints. 'We were paid in guineas, actually,' he says. 'It was two guineas here, three guineas there – much less than I had been earning before. I had to get rid of the car and bought a fifteen-year-old Volkswagen Beetle. But I was extremely happy.'

Henty says:

'My budget for the sports programme *Sports Parade* was just £15 a programme, so most of the contributors were lucky if they got a couple of quid. And that included Des.

'We took on a batch of sports reporters after advertising in the *Evening Argus*. There was a postman who did boxing, a chef and a solicitor – all different characters. The auditions were held in a very small outside broadcast studio at the Royal Pavilion and people trooped in and read from a bit of paper. They were not permanent jobs, just an opportunity to get into broadcasting. We couldn't pay them much, as I say, but we kept telling them that the experience was absolutely beyond their wildest dreams, it was priceless. They were on radio and in a sports programme.

'They were really very good. The postman was an excellent boxing commentator, doing local amateur bouts. The team were brilliant. There is no experience like it available today. Des went on to prove to the ultimate extent that there are thousands of good broadcasters out there if they get the chance to do it.

'I remember Des standing out – although at the time I must admit I did not see him becoming the major talent he has – but there was one early feature he did which showed he had something extra. Brighton had a bustling, hard-nut, bullet-headed striker – we called them centre forwards in those days – called Alex Dawson. Des latched onto him and we decided to do a sort of tribute to Alex Dawson. Des had the initiative to say, "Why do we not ring up Michael Parkinson and get a contribution from him." He was a major national figure and it's not something we would normally have done, but Des did it. And he got some good quotes from Michael Parkinson too.

'That was typical of Des's invention, and showed that he had wider thinking, too.'

Des was quick to spread his wings and put his huge comedic talents to good use by collaborating with Henty on a satirical show for Radio Brighton, called *How Lunchtime Is It?*

'It was typical of local radio at the time,' says Henty, 'that if you had an idea you could just get out there and do it. Des and I strung a few sketches together in front of a studio audience and put out this show called *How Lunchtime Is It?*

'When I say "studio audience" don't get the wrong impression. The studio was about the size of an average dining room but we wanted as many people as we could squeeze in to add to the feel. We would put together a 15-minute programme with topical gags and Des would also supply some of the voices. He's no bad mimic, but the man who was the real master of that was Peter Brackley. He clearly had hidden talent in that area.

'I'm not sure if any of those recordings still exist but I kept one, a special we did one Christmas which we called *How Yuletide Is It?* Des did a very funny stint about Christmas Day and one of his catchphrases was "It's your day, Mother, you must enjoy yourself". Of course it's probably the one day in the year when Mum is busier than ever, but Des would keep throwing in the catchphrase. It was really very funny stuff.

'If there's one quality which Des has continued to have to this day, it's his humour. There was no humour in sports broadcasting in those days, it was all done deadly seriously, but I like to think that we brought humour into it. In fact, there were a few innovations which we saw catch on elsewhere. We were the first, I believe, to broadcast a radio programme over the tannoy at a football ground. We put our show out over the speaker system at the Goldstone and called it "Goldstone Sound". I can recall us interviewing a balding referee called Roger Kirkpatrick who used to run backwards.'

Today Des has the benefit of autocues, and live feeds into his earpiece, video monitors, satellite communications and all of the latest technical gadgetry and wizardry. But in those days, doing the job meant something much more basic and down to earth. Stanley Allen adds:

'Des would remember that back at the studio they always wanted an interview, whatever match or event you were covering. They would shout out to you down the "can", "Go and get an interview with somebody." You rushed off with your Uher – it was a tape recorder basically – and you interviewed the captain or whoever, took it back to the station yourself, edited the tape and stuck it on the machine and played it.

'We'd go dashing back, hot from the event, get the old razor blade out and cut the tape to edit out the bits you didn't want and then play the finished version on the programme. It was a good grounding because we learned everything the hard way. We made mistakes, obviously, and it was fairly amateurish but it worked and people listened to it.

'Funnily enough, Peter Brackley was our producer at one point. Young Peter, as we all called him, because we were all quite a bit older than him. He was young but he knew his stuff. I don't suppose he would have expected to cross paths with Des years later in the circumstances that they had both become very successful.

'Unfortunately in those early days the whole thing went out on VHF/FM. It wasn't on Medium Wave, when in those days not many people had VHF sets, so we thought we weren't getting to a very large audience.'

Money was so tight on those little stations that the people who worked there had to go cap in hand to raise funds if they wanted to cover anything special. The Radio Brighton team were lucky if they saw a £5 note every now and then.

'If you got five quid you were lucky,' says Stanley.

'Usually it was two pounds. It was just something towards your beer money, it was bugger-all really. You did it mainly for the love of it.

'I was on the advisory council for Radio Brighton and when the local radio stations were launched by the Government, the Government funded half of the cost and the people who wanted local radio had to go out and raise the rest. We went round all the local councils saying can we have £100 towards Radio Brighton.

'There was a famous day in cricket, which is my thing, when Sussex won the semi-final of the then Gillette Cup and we decided we would like to run it from Lords for the final. So, they said, well you'll have to get some money to have a phone line. A Post Office line costs money.

'We went round with the hat more or less and got the money for a line and that was my first ever broadcast from Lords. Des was on the other end "cueing in". At that time he was doing a spell "cueing in" the programmes. You know the sort of thing, he'd tell you down the line . . . "We're coming to you in one minute . . ." That sort of thing.'

It's just as well the roles weren't reversed. Cricket has never been Des's strong point. Stanley remembers Des rising through the ranks after getting a call asking him up to London to do some part-time work for Radio Two.

'Then he got into television,' says Stanley.

'I'll never forget it. I was doing a cricket commentary at the County Ground when Des came in and said, "They want me to do a thing on the telly, but they want me to do cricket and I know nothing about it."

'We took him through an over and said that's the bones of it. We literally had to tell him how to bullshit his way through it, you know. I think he did very well, or at least he got away with it. And that was the start of his TV career.

'We lost touch a little after that, as our paths inevitably became farther and farther apart. But he was always an extremely nice person – he's not someone with any side to him at all – and we'd occasionally meet up in Brighton for a drink.

'I know in those early days he was browned off with insurance – talk about a square peg in a round hole. He was very droll and we'd all tell stories in the pub after our Monday night broadcasts. We really enjoyed ourselves in those days. It was a fun time and a great team.

'Both of us eventually got onto the network radio through sport but the difference between local radio and doing a short piece for Radio One or Two was incredible.

'One of the many things was that you weren't allowed to take your own tape recorder – you got an engineer who would carry the damn thing round for you, which was an incredible waste of money to my mind. But you might also get £100 and in those days you thought you were rolling in it.

'It was quite an eye-opener seeing how the network worked.'

Des worked long and hard to understand how the network worked – and to make it work for himself. After arriving at Broadcasting House with glowing references and a burning desire to succeed, Des almost fell at the first hurdle, though. His audition went OK, but didn't set the world on fire. He was about to be rejected out of hand, ironically because the management felt he lacked personality, but an old sweat called Angus Mackay recognized something in young Lynam and decided to give him a go. Mackay had tutored Eamon Andrews and he 'sat' on Des for two years, until one night, after work, he delivered his own ultimate accolade. With his arm around Des's shoulder as they left Broadcasting House for the pub, Mackay said simply, 'Not at all bad, old son, not bad at all.'

Des was on his way.

He was soon given the job of fronting Radio 2's *Sports Report* in addition to his other broadcast duties. He shone at the tragedy-hit Munich Olympics of 1972, when eleven Israeli athletes were taken hostage and killed.

His reports, filed back to London, caught the eye of BBC radio news bosses, and before long, Des was invited to join the team producing Radio 4's prestigious *Today* programme. The *Today* programme has become one of the great institutions of radio broadcasting, famed for putting politicians on the spot and never shirking the tough questions when a subject becomes a bit of a hot potato.

He spent eighteen months on *Today*, but recalls:

'It was at the time when Jack de Manio was just on the way out. John Timpson and Robert Robinson were there and I was sort of the third man – the Kim Philby of the piece. It was a bloody good year of learning, but I was knackered at the end of it.

'I knew that in current affairs I could never be a Robin Day or somebody like that, but I thought that if I stayed in sport I could probably get near the top of the business.'

One of the first to recognize Des's potential after his arrival at Broadcasting House was Alan Hart, the former head of BBC Sport. Alan, who subsequently left the BBC and now works for one of the Beeb's main sporting rivals, Eurosport, says:

'Des was an outstanding radio reporter. So many are clones of Brian Moore or clones of whoever is at the top at the time and there are very few really distinctive voices to be heard. Des had that.

'He then moved to TV and was a presenter of Sunday afternoon cricket on BBC2. This was his introduction to telly and he was not happy in front of camera. It obviously terrified him quite a lot and on one occasion he just dried up. He was introducing somebody from Lords, I think, and he could not remember his name at all. He just dried up.'

It's hard to imagine our Des – Mr Cool and Confident – quaking before the cameras but, as he himself says time and time again, 'I'm really quite shy and I've never really had the confidence people think I have.' That innate fear of failure, the fear of looking a fool which had probably been with him since his earliest schooldays with a rich, almost incomprehensible Irish accent, was not helped by the fact that his first television task was on the one sporting subject he knew least about – cricket.

However, a golden rule much loved by sports fans states that: Form is temporary – Class is permanent. It was famously and frequently applied to England football captain Alan Shearer when he suffered something of a goal drought during match after international match. It's a phrase that applies equally well to Desmond Michael Lynam. No one is more critical of Des than the man himself.

If he thinks a particular performance was lacklustre or below par he'll ring his rock of confidence, Rose, his partner, and ask: 'Did you see that? What did you think?' He often gets calls from his son Patrick, who again provides a welcome boost of confidence if a particular broadcast somehow, slightly, falls below what we have all come to expect from Des – which is perfection.

Not that his lapses are serious or frequent. Usually they are only perceived lapses, anyway, Des being a shy and sometimes insecure individual even after all his many years of success. The viewers at home will not have noticed a slightly off-colour remark or perhaps a note of frustration which Des fears might have slipped through his normally cool delivery.

Certainly in the early days of his fledgling broadcasting career goofs and gaffes and technical hiccups were expected, part and parcel of everyday life. They were all part of the learning curve that has made Des the consummate professional that he is today.

Alan Hart adds:

'He decided after that uncomfortable airing that he wanted to go back to radio where he had come from, and that's just what he did. He said he had gone into radio to enjoy life. He had a nice flat, with an MGB sports car at the door, and what more could he want? But I told him his future was in television.

'A couple of months later I tried again. *Nationwide* was still going and on Friday nights BBC Sport had a twenty-minute spot – a round-up programme of all the latest sports news – to do. I had already decided it was an ideal opportunity to try out talent and I reckoned Des would have as good a chance as anybody, if I could persuade him to give television another go.

'There were three presenters for the slot, Des being one, with Ron Pickering and Peter Walker the cricketer being the others. Des was persuaded to do the slot once every three weeks initially. I thought it was a good opportunity to try out these three people – two of whom fancied themselves as presenters and Des, who didn't.

'It only took two turns for me to realize that Des was back on form, much more comfortable than on his first experience, and that he was doing it well. We carried on with the experiment, but Des never looked back after that.

'I think the fact that he was working on autocue gave him more comfort and he was not ad-libbing.

'So many people are terrified of being in front of the camera. You are so conscious of the camera that you can't perform and that was what obviously happened the first time around. But the second time, all right he was on autocue, but it was as though he had moved on past the business of being frightened of the camera.'

A long-standing friend of Des, the legendary boxing commentator Reg Gutteridge, remembers how troubled the newcomer was in those early days in front of camera.

'I've known him for years and I worked with him several times when he was fronting that Sunday night show on BBC.

'I know when he first went into television that he was terribly nervous – and he showed it. For a time he was unsure whether he wanted to do it or not.

'You'd never know it now, of course. He's got the art that conceals the art really, hasn't he? He's probably still nervous but he makes it look as though he isn't. That's one of the things that I admire about him.'

That mastering of 'the art that conceals the art' didn't take Des long. Alan Hart says:

'Then, of course, he developed his own style and his own personality came through. He was always from the start Des Lynam – he was not trying to be Brian Moore or David Coleman. He was not trying to be Frank Bough.

'Broadcasters like that only come through once in a generation, certainly only one in a decade.

'You can count them on one hand – David Coleman, Frank Bough, Des Lynam – totally different people, all with this fantastic ability to communicate, and with the confidence to communicate, all with their own individual style, each one very different. Each surrounded by lots of other people who are good broadcasters but they just stood out above them.'

Having coaxed Des back into television broadcasting it was a very short space of time before it was clear that he had arrived, that he had imposed his own particular style on sports broadcasting.

'Women viewers were writing in in droves and we were aware that Des was reaching out to more than just sports fanatics,' says Hart.

'A lot of people thought Des was quite fanciable. It was something of a shock to all of us in the back room. We were sport and we never thought about things in that way. But all of a sudden Des was getting a mailbag of fan letters and he was beginning to get into the newspapers, but none of that seemed to go to his head. He was always very good company and very, very professional.

'It wasn't long after that that he began to host the *Sports Personality of the Year* awards before a live audience. It was clear that he had found his feet and his confidence had soared. He was now able to be himself and being without autocue didn't faze him. He was comfortable in front of a live audience just as he was in front of the camera.

'When we meet, which we do from time to time, he says thank you for giving me that opportunity and I say to him that it's great to see how his career has really flourished. I know whoever had been in charge of sport at the time would have found Des and brought him to a wider audience, but it's still nice for me to think that I was the one lucky enough to have been in the driving seat at the time, and to have spotted his potential.'

Now Des makes it all seem so easy that some people think that it really must be. But Hart is quick to dispel that view. He adds:

'Des's laid-back style might fool a few people into thinking well, if he's that laid back it must be easy. But that's not the case at all. It's just that Des cares very much about getting it right and he always did his homework.

'On a programme like *Grandstand*, like *Sportsnight*, you have to do your homework because if you are sitting there preening you will be found out very quickly. There's no one more discerning than sports fans and if you don't know your sport they will have you.'

It is one of the truisms of sporting life – almost a mantra to all great sportsmen and, more especially, their managers – that in life, the harder you work the luckier you get . . .

Hart comments: 'Radio was a fantastic stepping stone for Des. It was an environment where he was surrounded by people with immense sporting knowledge. I don't know of anyone coming through these days with a completely distinguished voice like Des.'

Des is the first to admit the slight shakiness of his introduction to television. Though slickly self-assured after some twenty years in front of the cameras, he recalls:

'Television worried me to death. I was camera shy. I had been perfectly happy in front of a microphone but live television is very difficult. You need six eyes and four pairs of ears and a split brain, really, to look comfortable while it's all going on. It took me some time to be comfortable at it. In fact, I wonder if I'm comfortable yet.

'When I first went to network radio there was a man called Angus Mackay running it. He told you in no uncertain terms whether you were doing it right, wrong or indifferently. While it hurt your pride a lot, it was bloody good in the long run.

'But when I moved to television there was absolutely no instruction, comment or anything about my performance at any time. No one told you how it should be done. I'd had a lot of advice in radio. Cliff Morgan was marvellous. But television hired you as the finished article.'

Still, he seems to have picked it up all right, doesn't he?

Another close friend of Des, the stalwart Wimbledon commentator Gerry Williams, witnessed Des's nervous television debut. He says:

'The first thing he presented when he got to television was, I think, on a Friday afternoon; a southern area opt-out before the *Six o'clock News*; and we all grouped round the monitor in the radio sports room to watch. Des looked nervous, which surprised us because we didn't think he would be nervous. We thought he could do it, but it showed that he was human too.

'When I first met him he had only just come up from Brighton and I had joined the BBC as their tennis correspondent from the *Daily Mail*. Des and the late Peter Jones were taking it in turns to present *Sports Report* and *Sport on Two* on the radio. Then, when it came to Wimbledon, Des was stuck out on court number 14 or somewhere like that.

'Well, some people who had already attained a certain star status would not be very keen to be stuck on court number 14 but Des didn't seem to mind. He had already established himself as presenter of *Sport on Two* and *Sports Report* so he could have been justified in feeling pushed out to the sidelines. It was report pieces as well, not commentary. Max Robertson and I and Fred Perry would be doing the main matches from the show courts.

'They would just say . . . "and over to Court 14 and Desmond Lynam. What's the latest . . ." and he would do forty-five seconds on the score in that match. It does say a lot about him that he was prepared to do that. Many people who have achieved high esteem in our business would think that was a bit undignified. But Desmond isn't precious in that sense.

'I am a huge fan of his as a bloke and as a professional. I think there's nobody quite like him.

'It did pay off for him, though. Maybe he had his eyes open to the fact that it could mean more involvement with Wimbledon later on, a better, more up front involvement. But when Des went to television we always knew, all of us who were there at the time, that Des would be a star.'

John Henty adds:

'He always needed a little push, quite frankly. He was a little uncertain. When he was first offered the job on Radio Two my wife, Sylvia, and I took Des with us up to Selhurst Park to watch Crystal Palace play. All the way home to Brighton we were persuading him to go for it, but he wasn't sure.

'I can't claim that I recognized his potential but he did have two major advantages which have always stood him in good stead. The first was an encyclopaedic knowledge of sport. When he went before a board (the BBC's appointments committee) he shocked them. He had a very, very good sports knowledge.

'Secondly there's the name. If you are going into sports journalism, Desmond Lynam is a good name to have. There are some names that go and some names that don't. Des Lynam goes with sport.'

Des, in fact, very nearly entered broadcasting using his middle name, Michael, rather than the familiar tag we have come to know and love. He says: 'I was going to change my name to Michael, my middle name, because I thought that, perhaps, Desmond would be seen as too posey. It's not in Ireland, it's a very Irish name. Anyway Cliff Morgan persuaded me not to do it. He said, "Now, don't call yourself Des, either. Call yourself Desmond. Keep your proper name up there and if people get to like you they'll shorten it for you." '

When Des eventually accepted the move and took the giant leap into the 'big time' he threw a party for his Brighton friends and colleagues which, again, says something about the man. John Henty adds:

'He had a celebration dinner for about twenty of us. It was a classy affair at a little French restaurant in Brighton, just to say farewell and to thank us all for being his pals and colleagues. It was a nice gesture. It's not something that everybody would do.

'Though he has gone on and made a magnificent career for himself he has always kept in touch and although he hasn't changed, other things have. Dramatically.

'When I went up to see him at his home in London, he offered to walk me back to Chiswick station along the river. Every single person was turning round and pointing. I just thought, "Well, that's part of the price of becoming so well known." He's not entirely comfortable with all of that. One of his passions is golf and he did tell me that the worst time of all is when he's on holiday and on the golf course, a little crowd of fifteen or so will gather round when he's on the first tee. Because you work in sport, he said, they all expect you to be Jack Nicklaus. He's far from that.

'Despite everything, though, he has kept his friends and he has not lost his roots.'

His 'radio roots' have certainly never been far from his heart and it was quite a coup for Radio 2 when they coaxed him back into the presenter's chair for a prime Friday night drive-time slot at the beginning of 1999.

'Fed up with work; fed up with the traffic; fed up with the

housework. For the next couple of hours come to Desmond. I'll take care of you. Personally,' he intones. He seems more relaxed, more natural than on *Match of the Day*, even. In his low, even timbre he introduces 'nice' middle-of-the-road stuff like Joe Jackson and Wham, or Bob Dylan classics – raising the voice an octave here, dropping it there, in a verbal equivalent of his on-screen eyebrow gymnastics.

Somehow, there's a cosy feeling that this is home for Des. It's certainly where the heart is.

4

All Sports and Grass Courts

'You'll never see bigger, taller or stronger people. It's really extraordinary to be ordinary.'

– Des on the Olympics

Still a relative 'new boy' at the BBC, Des was delighted to be part of the radio broadcasting team covering the Olympic Games from Munich in 1972. It was always going to be an exciting event and a great chance to prove yourself in one of the most demanding arenas for any journalist, whether broadcast or print media. Ask anyone who's ever covered an Olympic Games and they'll bend your ear, if you let them, complaining about the long hours, the difficulties of getting to and from all the different locations, the nightmare of keeping track of so many varied events and the fear of being in the wrong place at the wrong time and missing a breaking news story.

As far as his career was concerned, Des Lynam was definitely in the right place at the right time when he flew out to Germany for the 1972 'Games of Peace and Joy' as the Munich Olympics were officially declared. The intention had been to wipe out the bitter memories of Hitler's showpiece 'Aryan' Games in Berlin in 1936 which, since the Second World War, had become something of an embarrassment both to the German people and the Olympic movement.

What followed, though, was the most dramatic and tragic Olympics in history. The games, seen by an estimated audience of more than 900 million around the globe, was chosen by a Palestinian terrorist group calling themselves Black September to commit an act of atrocity which reverberated around a shocked world. On 5 September, masked gunmen from the terrorist organization broke into the Israeli living quarters in the Olympic village, sited just north of the city. Two Israeli athletes were killed and nine more were taken hostage. Sadly, all were to die.

Because the theme of the games had been 'Peace and Joy', the games were policed by volunteers armed only with walkie-talkies. Guard dogs and barbed wire fences were forbidden and the Olympic Village's security fence, over which the Black September killers swarmed, was just 6 feet high. No one had wanted to raise the spectre of athletes – Israeli or otherwise – behind barbed wire, in camps patrolled by dogs and armed men. The memories from the war years were just too painful. It was a genuinely thoughtful piece of planning which the terror-ists exploited with all their cunning brutality.

After killing the two athletes in the initial attack, the gunmen demanded a police helicopter to take them and their hostages to an airfield where they wanted a fully-fuelled jet made available to fly them to freedom. The authorities acquiesced and the gunmen and their captives were flown to the military airfield of Furstenfeld, where an airliner was waiting.

But as the terrorists and their hostages were being transferred across the dark tarmac from the helicopter to the jet, the German authorities struck. During the firefight which erupted, the nine Israeli hostages were killed and all but two of the Black September terrorists died, along with one policeman.

The bloody mayhem was terrible and the loss of life truly tragic. But as a story it was world news; one of the biggest stories a journalist would ever be involved in no matter how long a career they had. It made no odds if you were a sports journo or a hard news man, the massacre of the Israeli athletes overshadowed everything else. In circumstances like that, careers can be made or broken. Though naturally filled with revulsion at what had happened, the reporters suddenly found they had a massive job to do. Their adrenalin would have been running as high as any gold medal prospect waiting for the start.

Des, quite naturally, became embroiled in the scramble to find out what was going on; what had happened; reporting the carnage of the killings themselves; the shocking aftermath. How had the terrorists been able to accomplish this terrible deed so easily? What would happen to the Games? How were the other athletes going to react? There were a thousand and one questions that needed to be answered.

'It was total chaos,' recalls one former BBC man.

'Nobody could even have imagined such a thing happening but suddenly we were faced with the biggest story of a lifetime. Des was working for radio at the time and he handled it all in a very professional manner. We were all shocked but we had to concentrate on the news. Naturally the Games were suspended, although they did eventually continue after a lot of political negotiation, as it was felt that to abandon the Games would have been seen as a victory for terrorism.'

The Games continued in sombre mood and the tragedy overshadowed some remarkable personal feats. American swimmer Mark Spitz made history in the pool by winning an extraordinary seven gold medals, but the real darling of the Games was a pixie-like gymnast from the Soviet Union by the name of Olga Korbut. Her spectacular routines and diminutive figure really caught the public imagination as everyone struggled to get to grips with the Olympic movement's blackest hour.

Des was judged by his BBC bosses to have been another star performer. He was adjudged to have handled himself so well at the heart of such a major tragedy that when he returned to Broadcasting House there were moves to lure him away from sport into the hard-headed world of news and current affairs. 'It's more important than sport,' he was told. He resisted, of course. Des told the head of radio news: 'It might be more important than sport to you, but it's not to me.' Apart from a stint with the hard-hitting *Today* programme on Radio 4, Des has remained primarily a sports man, but he was certainly flattered that his handling of the crisis had been recognized as cool and professional.

The hallmarks, indeed, of what have marked his career ever since.

When he embarks on the journey to the other side of the world for the Sydney Olympics in 2000, Des will complete a remarkable odyssey embracing eight Olympic Games since that traumatic start in Munich. This time, however, he will not be representing the BBC. Bosses at the Beeb were devastated when he signed for ITV in August 1999 after thirty years with the Corporation. There had long been whispers, not that he was about to desert the BBC for a multi-million-pound deal with Sky, but just that he wanted to move on in his life and career. Cerainly he was expected to do the Sydney Olympics and, probably, to stay on for the next World Cup in 2002, after which he would call it a day. Instead, he joined ITV, frustrated at the lack of live soccer on the BBC.

In Montreal, where the next Games were held in 1976, he was still mainly commentating for BBC radio on boxing. But, even at that stage, no one doubted his ability to get to the people who mattered. One former BBC executive recalls:

'Montreal was the first time I had met Des. I'll never forget it. There are always press conferences and that sort of thing but it can be a bit of a nightmare to get hold of the star names for a quiet chat when you need them.

'I was on my way through the media centre or the Olympic Village, I can't remember which, looking for someone for the television sports report and stood waiting for a lift. When it arrived on my floor the door opened and out walked Des Lynam deep in conversation with George Foreman – along with Ali and Frasier one of the biggest names in world boxing. I knew of Des, he had already gained a bit of a reputation, but I didn't really know him. It was a couple of years later when he moved across to television that we became good mates.'

But the boxing events at Montreal were lacklustre to say the least. Again there had been controversy, with twenty-two African nations boycotting the Games because of the presence of New Zealand – a country which proudly maintained its sporting links with South Africa while other nations had frozen the apartheid regime out of world sport. Boxing and the long distance races suffered most from the boycott but, as always, there was plenty of excitement in other fields. This was the Games when fourteen-year-old Nadia Comaneci scored the first perfect ten in Olympic history on the very first day of her gymnastic performance. She went on to be awarded five further tens on her way to three gold medals.

Des had really left radio for the 'glamour' of TV by the start of the 1980 Olympics in Moscow. And it turned out to be yet another Games rocked by controversy, ensuring that coverage didn't just make the sports pages and broadcasts, but ended up as front-page or lead-item news.

American President Jimmy Carter withdrew the US team from the Games in protest against the Soviet invasion and continued occupation of Afghanistan. Against a background of heavy political and diplomatic turmoil, most other European countries dropped out of the Games but the British athletes went to Moscow, despite heavy hints from the Prime Minister Margaret Thatcher that they, too, should withdraw.

'Everyone in the BBC team was nervous about the Moscow Olympics,' says the former executive.

'Thatcher didn't want our athletes to go and the presence of the BBC in that sort of environment was obviously polit-ically sensitive. There were the usual accusations that we were being anti-Government and all that crap.

'Des wasn't the lead presenter but he was as well aware of the difficult political situation we were in as anyone. A sort of compromise had to be worked out whereby the sports team would provide material for the news programmes, especially *Nationwide*.

'We were all being extra careful but then the most bizarre story broke. Someone accused the Russians of opening the stadium doors when their javelin throwers were in action, to create a wind inside the stadium which would assist the flight of their javelins and give them an advantage. When the next competitors took to the field, they would shut the doors again.

'The story had broken on the UPI wire service, but we hadn't had any confirmation from Reuters where we would normally look to get some sort of authenticity about a story like that. I had a chat with Des about it and we were both very dubious so I checked it out by taking a very senior figure from the International Olympic Committee out to dinner. He assured me it was all nonsense and that someone at the IOC had fallen out with the Russians and leaked the story to UPI to get at them.

'When we put our news report together, instead of putting this story up the front as a lead item, I relegated it to the back and made sure that it was described as something reported by a wire service not as fact.

'I called Broadcasting House the following morning with some trepidation and asked if they were happy with the previous night's news report only to get an earful. The news guy went bananas shouting that this story was on the front page of the *Daily Mail* and in every national newspaper. Well, we had taken the trouble to check it out at the highest level so I was pretty annoyed myself. What I said doesn't bear repeating. However, the story of how the Russians cheated by opening the stadium doors during the javelin became part of Olympic folklore. Des and I were just glad that, as professionals, we hadn't endorsed it because it was plainly wrong.'

Something else happened, though, during the Moscow Olympics which ultimately had a significant effect on Des's career. Frank Bough, ace face and number one man for the big event suffered from what those on the ground can only recall as 'a breakdown'. It was the beginning of the end of Bough's tenure as top dog in sport and left a huge opening for someone else whose style and coolness under pressure had already caught the eye. Desmond Michael Lynam.

The former BBC man recalls:

'Bough had a nervous breakdown, simple as that. Mind you, we were living in an absolute state – the conditions we had over there were appalling. The worst I ever encountered in a major capital and without doubt the worst we had at any Olympics.

'We were also in the midst of a technical nightmare. We had some great guys working in the field but in those days the equipment was nowhere near as sophisticated as you find today. You operated on a wing and a prayer sometimes. There could be breakdowns or sudden losses of transmission.

'The presenters had to be mentally quick on their feet. At that time Frank was not on the top of his game. We had to write every single word for him and pray that there wouldn't be a problem where he would have to fill.

'One of Des's great qualities has always been that he will remain calm under pressure and fill the gaps. If you have a breakdown he can talk, read other reports, discuss things . . . He takes it all in his stride.'

Back home the BBC's coverage seemed, as ever, knitted together seamlessly. But Bough's breakdown was not overlooked and, in a sense, the knives were out.

Mike Murphy, who was editor of *Grandstand* in the years after the Moscow Olympics, recalls how a gap suddenly opened up and Des was in with the predatory instinct of Michael Owen. He says:

'We were running out of patience with Frank on the *Grandstand* team. He had commitments to *Nationwide* every Friday which seemed to occupy an undue amount of his attention. Then one day he just announced to us that he was leaving sport to become the lead presenter on the new

Breakfastime show which was starting up.

'At the same time there was also a feeling that Coleman – who will always remain one of the greats of sports broadcasting – had begun to lose his edge. Some people wondered whether or not he could hold it all together for much longer. Remember, there was huge pressure on the shoulders of anyone in that live *Grandstand* hot seat.

'Anyway, with Bough's sudden departure, well that was "Open Sesame" for Des.

'Coleman made a bit of a comeback as the lead presenter on *Grandstand* with Des as the second man. I think Coleman did Saturday *Grandstand* and Des fronted Sunday *Grandstand* whenever we did that.

'Des's approach was like a breath of fresh air. In the BBC they have a set of rules which everyone is expected to conform to. There was a format and individuals are moulded to that. But Des was and still is his own man. He wanted to do things his way. His style was not to talk down to the viewers but to say something like, "Come into my parlour and let me show you what's happening." '

Viewers certainly liked Des's way of doing things and it was no surprise to the backroom boys at the Beeb when he was handed the number one position with the *Grandstand* team.

By 1982, Des was comfortably installed as presenter of Sunday *Grandstand*, with some Saturdays spent filling in for Coleman. He was, by this time, also presenting *Sportswide* – part of the popular *Nationwide* news and current events programme – on Friday nights and fitting in some of the bigger sports events into his increasingly hectic schedule.

His busy day usually began with a breakfast of porridge and a vitamin tablet and a good read of four or five newspapers to make sure he was fully conversant with events of the day, especially, of course, whatever was happening in sport. On *Grandstand* days he liked to arrive at the studios nice and early – around 10.00 am – to put in the preparation which has always marked his professional approach. With a five-hour live programme ahead, you wouldn't want to leave everything to chance.

I don't know about you, but in our house *Grandstand* – Saturday *Grandstand* especially – was required viewing every week. Just as we had to go to church every Sunday morning, we had to sit round the television every Saturday afternoon watching the football results coming up on the teleprinter. It was a family occasion, especially on those cold, wet, winter Saturdays when we huddled round a blazing coal fire dreaming that within the next thirty minutes we might 'come up on the pools'.

Firstly I remember David Coleman keeping us entertained on our black and white set through the entire afternoon whenever the weather was so foul we couldn't escape outdoors to play we also had football. Then Frank Bough and Des Lynam. There was competition, of course. Dickie Davies's *World of Sport* over on ITV was, at that time, throughout the 1970s, the housewives' favourite. Partly because Dickie exuded the sort of moustachioed charm Des was to inherit in later years and partly because housewives everywhere loved the grunt-and-groan bouts of wrestling screened every Saturday.

Anyway, sometimes it was a close-run thing whether we watched the wrestling on ITV's *World of Sport* or the horse racing followed by the footie results on BBC1's *Grandstand*.

In 1984, just before the Games, Des flew out to Los Angeles, where the legacy of America's Moscow boycott cast a shadow over the proceedings. Inevitably, the Russian team decided not to attend as an act of revenge. Still, once again there were some individual highlights to cherish. Carl Lewis lived up to the achievements of the legendary Jesse Owens by grabbing gold in the 100 metres, 200 metres, the long jump and the 4 x 100 metres relay. And the hot favourite for the women's 3000 metres event was sent sensationally tumbling out of the race after tangling with the young, barefooted, South African runner, Zola Budd.

Des spent four days in LA putting a programme together before dashing back to London for a punishing marathon stint, working almost night and day at Television Centre as the key Olympics link man. He recalls: 'I made a programme in Los

71

Angeles and flew home straight into a day's *Grandstand* followed by the opening ceremony of the Olympics.'

It was to be a defining period in Des's career. Working with the then *Grandstand* editor, John Philips, Des was allowed to really show his unique style. He says: 'We had the same approach. Instead of selling the Olympics we slightly under-played it. We made jokes about synchronized swimming or whatever without demeaning the great events. I think it was about then that people started to think, "This boy's not so bad." '

This was also the year that Des finally got the coveted Saturday *Grandstand* seat all to himself. He was made full-time *Grandstand* host when the legendary Coleman decided to stand down. Prior to that the pair had been sharing the *Grandstand* duties in rotation.

By 1988 the Games had moved across the world to Seoul in Korea – but controversy had not been left far behind. The Canadian 100-metres world-record-holder Ben Johnson was stripped of his gold medal in disgrace after he failed a drugs test.

Des was presenting live to camera as the shocking news began to filter through. With his excellent news sense, Des real-ized what a terrific story was unfolding as soon as he saw the first reports coming through on the news wires. Without miss-ing a beat he was able to bring viewers instantly up to speed with the dramatic developments. The folks back home knew the details almost as soon as the members of the IOC.

There was also a much-needed injection of glamour at the Seoul Games which lit up the twinkle in Des's eye. Florence Griffith-Joyner, the stunning American sprinter, had most commentators tripping over their tongues as she sped to glory in both the 100 metres and 200 metres, wearing her trademark flashy bodysuits and incredibly long painted fingernails.

An air of true Olympian harmony had settled over the Games by the time Barcelona played host in 1992. The political turmoil of previous events had mostly been resolved; South Africa was back in the international fold and countries like Cuba, North Korea and Ethiopia had ended their long-standing boycotts of the Games.

The Games began with a little disharmony for Des, however, as he took exception to an inaccurate, but seemingly harmless, piece of reporting in the *Daily Mirror*. What followed was a classic example of just how protective Des can be about his image and/or reputation. Any slight, no matter how small, has always brought a reaction.

In this instance the object of Des's ire was showbusiness reporter Nigel Pauley, who had been dispatched to interview the great man for a preview piece on the Olympics. It was an encounter which almost cost him his job. Pauley, now showbusiness editor of the *Daily Star*, recalls:

'I always thought of Des Lynam as a top bloke – Mr Happy-Go-Lucky, and totally laid back. But I was in for a shock.

'I was asked to write a piece for the *Mirror*'s *TV Weekly* section and I finally managed to get a few minutes with Des up at TV Centre as he walked from one building to another. It wasn't ideal but all I needed was a brief chat.

'The piece went in on the Saturday. It was an innocuous few paragraphs about Des taking Spanish lessons before going to Barcelona, and someone else had written in that he owned a racehorse, that sort of thing. I must admit there were a couple of inaccuracies, like his age was wrong, but these things happen.

'By Monday morning there was a fax on editor Richard Stott's desk from Barcelona from an angry Mr Lynam criticizing the piece in about six different ways. He said that he wasn't taking lessons in Spanish because he could already speak the language fluently, but he had been "brushing up" on the subject. He didn't own a racehorse, but he had had a share in one. I couldn't believe he had found the time in Barcelona to go through the *Daily Mirror* to find such a small, innocuous article about himself, and to take such great exception to such minor points.

'Stott went ballistic and said there was no room on his newspaper for me. I had to sneak into the office every day for the next three months and use the pseudonym Paul Stanley for byline purposes as well as constantly avoiding the editor. Finally I was reprieved on a Friday night, and on the Saturday Stott was sacked himself.

'I mean, we all think Des is great but that Mr Nice Guy image that people have, the happy-go-lucky image thing, hides a man who's easily offended. It was the sort of reaction you might expect from a showbiz luvvie. It wasn't as though I was saying anything nasty about him.'

Although the showbusiness writer was amazed at Des's swift attack on him, pals in television would not be surprised. He has always been quick to react when there's something he doesn't like. And there are other examples of Des being quick off the mark to put the record straight if something upsets him.

Early in 1999 a newspaper columnist suggested that Des had 'lost his cool' after being introduced at a showbusiness bash as the man who turned women on. Unfortunately the words '. . . to soccer on television' should have been part of this introduction. A rapid phone call from Des, pointing out that far from losing his cool he had, in fact, thought the episode very funny, soon saw the error being corrected in the newspaper column.

'If he believes in something he doesn't hold back,' says one pal. 'If he has got something to say he doesn't mind who he says it to and how loudly he has to say it. Like anyone, he would be quick to react to a criticism, whether intended or implied – if he felt it was unjustified. But something that was just plain wrong would be like a red rag to a bull. He's very professional himself – some people would say a perfectionist – and he would like others to do their jobs in a professional way too.'

When the crowds gathered in Atlanta, Georgia, on 4 August 1996, the sight of Muhammad Ali lighting the Olympic flame was more poignant for Des than the average sports fan. Des has been a lifelong admirer of the boxer they called 'the Greatest' but who was by then debilitated with Parkinson's disease.

The summer of '96 was a long one for Des and the BBC sports team. There had been all the drama and excitement of the European football championships in our own back yard, the annual Wimbledon tennis tournament, and then it was time to race across the Atlantic for the Olympics in Atlanta.

But Des never tires of the Olympics. He once described walking through an Olympic village as an amazing experience. He said: 'You'll never see bigger, taller, or stronger people. It's really extraordinary to be ordinary.'

Another of Des's sporting passions is the annual fortnightly gathering in a south-west London suburb at the All England Croquet and Tennis Club for the Holy Grail of tennis – the Wimbledon Championships. Des loves both watching and playing the game. Throughout the 1980s he was thrilled to bring into Britain's households – first through radio and then on television – the all-time greats of the game like John McEnroe, Jimmy Connors, Arthur Ashe and Bjorn Borg. They were followed by great champions like Stefan Edberg, Boris Becker and Michael Stich.

Surely it is only coincidence that in the period Des Lynam has been presenting tennis from Wimbledon the game has been transformed from an elitist sport to a genuine people's game, with crowds who, instead of just clapping politely and consuming over-priced strawberries, now shout and cheer and add the excitement which passionate support gives to these highly skilful duels between superbly-honed athletes.

Legendary Wimbledon figure Gerry Williams has been a friend of Des's for some twenty years and, from the mid 1980s onwards, the pair formed a highly successful Wimbledon doubles team. Their blend of informed analysis, interviews and highlights mixed with large doses of sharp wit and humour saw them dubbed the most popular team since Tom and Jerry. Sometimes they were more like Morecambe and Wise.

And it certainly paid off.

Gerry recalls:

'Des and I did eight or nine years of Wimbledon together on television and we did radio together for about eight years before that. He's the best, isn't he?

We used to go and eat after a hard day at Wimbledon, a few of us. There was an Indian restaurant at the top of the hill which we used to like.'

The pair were brought together at just the right time, as the BBC injected some new life into their broadcasts of the event. Gerry says:

'Bob Burrows was our boss in those days and he was responsible for the overnight transformation of the radio coverage of Wimbledon. At a stroke he changed it from being a very pedantic sort of thing and he turned it into a big production. Des was a very significant part of that.

'Eventually Des went to television and we always knew, all of us who were there at the time, that Des would be a star. We had a wonderful staff with Peter Jones, Brian Butler, Chris Martin Jenkins, Chris Robertson and Derek Thompson – it was just an amazing team. I don't think there has been another like it.

'I went plodding on at radio because I had a nice job there and I went around the world but I always felt that I could do television. After a time, Des said to me, "I don't think you'd like it here, there are too many hard noses." He knew that I wasn't into the hard-drinking and four-letter word in every other sentence kind of scene. Then, after a few years, he called and said it had changed a lot and that there were a lot of young people that I would get on with. Anyway, I got my chance and I went to television, too.

'Funnily enough I did the first two years of *Match of the Day* from Wimbledon – not the football – with David Vine but hardly anyone seems to remember that. It just didn't make an impression. Then they put Des and me together and it just clicked right away.'

Their banter and humour soon became cult viewing. The pair even featured on the award-winning satirical puppet show *Spitting Image*.

Gerry recalls:

'Jonathan Martin, who was head of sport, was a bit uneasy at some of the lightheartedness, some of the banter we used to indulge in but it worked. We never sat down and said let's do this or that, it just developed. Des has said many, many times, "Gerry and I just love sport and we don't think it's the start of World War Three." Jonathan didn't quite understand . . .

'We did not just sit and review points, although we did analyse games, we actually got up to some quite funny things as well. It became cult viewing. We were even featured on *Spitting Image* and Terry Wogan, every morning on his radio show, would say, "Did you see those two at it again last night." It was very generous of him because it added to the feeling that ours was a special partnership.

'We were even being given ideas from the Wimbledon committee. Once Chris Gorringe phoned up and said, "We can put your names on the scoreboard, if you want, something like Lynam beats Williams six-love, six-love."

'We were getting huge audiences and all sorts of people were writing about what we were doing. But not everybody liked it, of course. I remember some lady in one of the tabloids called me Wally of the Week once; but the point was it was natural for Des and I to do those things. That's how we are. We liked to have a little rub at each other.

'There were some great gags. You got the impression usually that Des had the last laugh in these things. I was the fall guy to some extent. One night our producer, Graham Fry, said to me, "Hey, we have got an idea for tonight and we think it's about time you got your own back on Des."

'In the middle of the tennis *Match of the Day* we had to

show some football – I can't remember if it was the World Cup, but there was some big football match on – and anyway we did, like, half an hour of tennis and then Des linked into the football and then came back for more tennis.

'Des had apparently said to Graham Fry: "I'll get Gerry tonight because when we come back to the tennis after the football, I'll ask him for an opinion on one of the Paraguayan players," or something like that, "and he won't have a clue what I'm talking about and it'll be a bit of a laugh."

'So Graham Fry said he's gonna do this, and the player's name is so-and-so. I arranged to call Barry Davies and said, "Barry, tell me everything there is to know about so-and-so."

'When we did this live at night, Des did the introduction to the football and afterwards it was back to Wimbledon. When we came back on, he said "What do you think of so-and-so, Gerry?" meaning this player. They left the camera on Des's face – and they said it was an absolute picture. Instead of floundering away I said, "Well, when he played for Cadiz, or whatever it was, he was a left-sided midfielder but, of course, he's got this wonderful peripheral vision and he can do these jinking runs down the wing and he can cut inside . . ." And, of course, Des's face was ashen.

'We often did things like that.

'He left me once, stuck up at the top of one of those great hoists we used for overhead camera shots. It was a bit of a cheat, actually. We shot it in the afternoon, but he gave the impression that he had left me up in one of those hoists overnight.

'Another one was our take-off of the newsreaders. You know how newsreaders often end programmes shuffling their notes and putting pens conspicuously away, so I said we should take that off. We did and we did it ever so theatrically one night. We had also got the studio set up for this.

'They dimmed the lights but left our sound up and I said, "Well, that's a good day but our producer just drives me up the wall." Des replied, "Oh, he's hopeless." I said, "Come on, let's pop up the road and get a pizza," and that was how it ended. The next morning when we got to Wimbledon there were these piles of pizzas from the local pizza shop. All the BBC staff had a free lunch.'

Des has created one or two memorable Wimbledon moments of his own. He once watched an enraged McEnroe throwing a particularly nasty tantrum on court and he turned to the camera and said: 'If I told you what I thought of that little lot, I'd probably get the sack.' On the frequent rainy days he has to summon all his skills to keep things moving, from ancient replays of Borg or Connors to the prospects of play re-starting in whatever match is being held up. In 1999, with eleven hours of airtime to fill each day, torrential downpours interrupted play for three long days. On one occasion, Des announced: 'This is live rain you are watching, not recorded rain.' During another look around the sodden courts he said: 'All we need is a celebrity chef to make this a hit, or some redecorating of the Centre Court, or some gardening with Charlie Dimmock.' Arthur Smith, who wrote *My Summer with Des*, reckons that on those occasions he turns into 'a kind of housewives' Samuel Beckett'.

Bosses at the BBC feared some of the irreverence of Des's daily duets with Gerry Williams might upset committee members at the famously stuffy club. But, instead, they loved the Des and Gerry double act. Gerry adds:

'I saw Buzzer Haddingham, who used to be chairman of Wimbledon, a while back and he said he sometimes sat down and remembered some of the things Des and I did and had a little chuckle. There was one year when we closed our Wimbledon fortnight with the camera behind us, as we were walking out to the car park, our hands deep in our pockets. The conversation Des and I had went something like this:

' "Went well this fortnight, Des."

' "Yeah, yes it did."

' "Buzzer did well, didn't he?"

' "Buzzer," said Des. "Buzzer . . . ?"

' "You know, Buzzer Haddingham, the chairman . . . "

'They just let it fade. It wasn't particularly clever, but it was unusual and people have remembered it.'

Gerry can't resist the opportunity to have a last light-hearted pop at Des. He says: 'I was usually busy doing commentaries and interviews all day. Desmond, of course, would come in later, swanning around, and then we used to get together with Graham Fry and say, "Right, what are we going to do tonight?" '

But he adds quickly:

'Desmond has a very clear mind about what works on television. I would come up with an idea and Des would say, "No that won't work." And then an hour later I'd get back from doing an interview or doing a commentary on a match and Des would say, "You know that idea of yours? If we did it this way it would work." I have often said that if he hadn't been a television performer he could have been a theatrical producer. He's got a very smart idea of what you can do.

'I remember the BBC putting on some very, very high-class do at the Dorchester one night. They had hired two or three quite well known entertainers and there were some very high-profile, powerful figures there from television and sport and the FA and all that. I asked Des if we couldn't do something and he said, "Yes, let's." So we rewrote the words to that Maurice Chevalier song, "Yes, I Remember It Well", so that it included all sorts of BBC jokes, jokes about the FA, jokes about the players we knew were going to be there. They gave us a professional pianist and we performed it.

'It went down terribly well. In fact, we were asked to do it again but we decided it had worked once and that it was a good idea not to do it again.'

5

A Ladies' Man

Busts and bosoms have I known
Of various shapes and sizes
From grievous disappointments
To jubilant surprises

Anon

In the spring of 1998, as the prospect of a new millennium seemed to create an umbrella of optimism for us all, everything appeared particularly rosy in the world of Des Lynam. He was firmly established as television's man for all seasons on a contract worth £2 million over four years; advertisers were falling over themselves to court 'Dishy Des', whose authority or self-parody – available in equal measure for suitable sums – could sell us anything from deodorant to garden fertilizer; he was a 'mate' to the millions of football fans in pubs around the country and a pin-up to 'ladies of a certain age' throughout the land.

Moreover, there was the exciting prospect of the World Cup in France looming, with Des to guide us through the inevitable traumas of England and Scotland's bids to progress in the tournament.

Behind the scenes, however, trouble was building up in Des's private life. He was in the midst of a torrid affair with a neighbour – an attractive red-headed widow – whom he wooed and pursued relentlessly in spite of the fact that he had been with his partner, Rose Diamond, for more than fourteen years.

It would turn out to be almost more than the women of Middle England could bear. Secretly, it is what they had hoped for – that behind the knowing winks and seductive smile there really was a bit of a devil; a womanizing rogue in a Prince Charming package.

The affair itself was more like a plot from a Jilly Cooper novel than a Mills and Boon romance. Tall, handsome, television personality, worshipped by millions, falls for alluring, wealthy widow. The pair embark on a steamy affair, driven by over-whelming passion to ignore the dangers. There are long, linger-ing champagne lunches at the finest restaurants; illicit liaisons in posh hotels; hot sexual encounters that were always more urgent than loving.

Finally, in a dramatic climax, the hero is confronted with the one dilemma he did not want to face, but one which was inevitable. His betrayal is about to be exposed to the world, possibly in front of an audience of millions during the World Cup, the highpoint of his working achievement. He must choose between the two women who are rivals for his affections – the woman he adores and has spent so many years with, or the exciting red-head who has ignited frenzied emotions so long kept in check. Such drama.

But this was not the world of fiction where no one gets hurt. The reality was that Des had created a painful mess by embark-ing on a two-year affair. For years he had had to cope with the 'Dishy Des' tag, something which secretly pleased him yet left him feeling embarrassed at the same time. Suddenly he was living up to his reputation as a smooth-talking ladies' man whose flirtatious manner could charm the birds from the trees.

By the start of the World Cup in France, details of his romance were known by at least one newspaper but he remained blind to the risks. Incredibly he had asked his lover, the glamorous Laura Ewing, to join him in Paris where he was leading the BBC's commentary team. But when he was confronted outside Laura's hotel after spending the night with her, by a reporter from the *Sun*, the affair was doomed. He finally realized the game was up, although the *Sun* agreed not to run the story.

Having escaped public exposure, Des decided on drastic action. He abandoned Laura and chose to work things out with Rose. It's hard to imagine the pain that Rose felt – she has always shied away from the glare of publicity and has never been keen to stand under the spotlight with Des. Indeed, it came as a surprise to many when his relationship with Rose was first reported in a newspaper in 1996 – some twelve years after they had first become an item – such was her desire to remain in the background. But Laura's agony and bitterness at the way in which the eternal triangle had fractured was revealed when she angrily told her story to two newspapers, the *Mail on Sunday* and the *News of the World*, just two months later.

She felt betrayed and let down by the man she loved. He dropped her like a hot stone, she says, when his comfortable lifestyle was threatened and left her to face the financial and emotional consequences of their doomed affair alone. The headlines were Laura's revenge on Des for the way he had treated her. 'Des Lynam was my lover . . . he promised to leave his partner but he just used me and then abandoned me,' said the *Mail on Sunday*.

The *News of the World* was, typically, more robust. 'Des played a blinder in bed then he dashed off to cover Belgium v Mexico,' revealed one headline. 'He was voted Britain's best neighbour but had six-times-a-night frolics with widow next door,' screamed another. Of course, the story was enthusiastically followed up by Britain's remaining tabloids and even papers like *The Times* and the *Sunday Telegraph* reported the story and carried Des's contrite, but brief, reaction.

Publicist Max Clifford, who brokered the deal between Laura Ewing and the newspapers, said: 'Des conned Laura. He got her to move out of her home and set up in a new place where she thought they would be together. But it didn't happen and she is very upset about it. Des has been a coward. Basically Des has been scoring at home and away but now, I suppose, he is staying at home. From everything that has been said I would imagine there are other skeletons in Des's cupboard. He just seems to be that way inclined.'

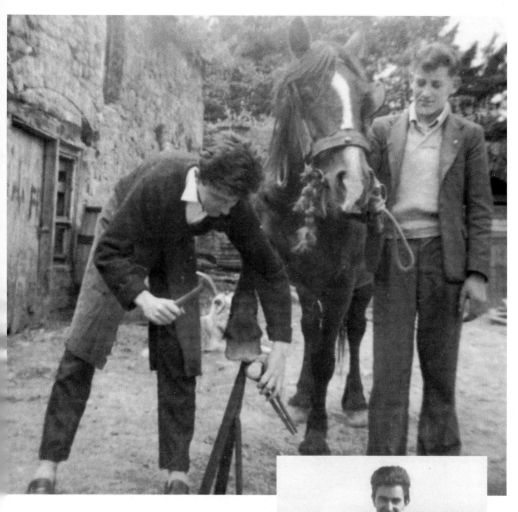

HORSE SENSE: Des follows family tradition by shoeing a horse on holiday in Ireland. His uncle was the last blacksmith in Ennis.

TALL GUY: As a young man, Des was tall and handsome – though rather skinny.

RADIO DAYS: A young Des Lynam (back row, fourth from left) with colleagues from his first broadcasting job at Radio Brighton.

(STANLEY ALLEN)

MAN FOR ALL SEASONS: Des poses with an outside broadcast camera before Wimbledon in 1986.

(UNIVERSAL PICTORIAL PRESS)

OLD PALS ACT: Des shares a joke with Jimmy Hill.

(REX FEATURES)

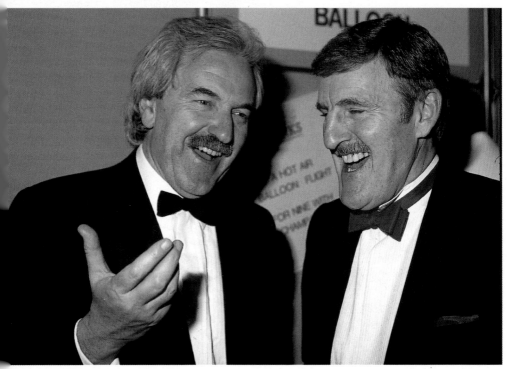

TOP TEAM: The Beeb's Cup Final 'back four' comprising (right to left) Des, John Motson, Trevor Brooking and Alan Hansen.

(ALLSPORT)

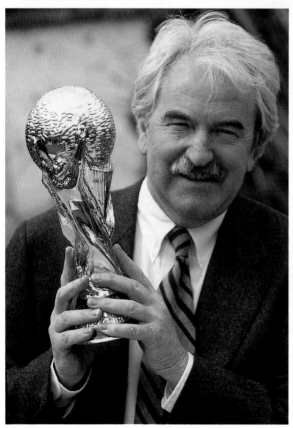

UP FOR THE CUP: Des holds the 'Holy Grail' of world soccer – the fabulous World Cup trophy.

(REX FEATURES)

GOOD SPORT: Des was the BBC's greatest supporter for many years.

(UNIVERSAL PICTORIAL PRESS)

IT MUST BE GLOVE: Boxing fan Des meets modern ringmaster 'Prince' Naseem Hamed.

(UNIVERSAL PICTORIAL PRESS)

KNOCKOUT: Des and his partner Rose with Britain's favourite heavyweight, Henry Cooper, and his wife.

(MIRROR SYNDICATION INTERNATIONAL)

BOXING CLEVER: Desmond's first sporting love is boxing.
Here he's pictured clowning around in 1990.

AND THE WINNER IS ...
Des arriving at the BAFTAs
where he picked up an award
for best TV sports presenter.

(REX FEATURES)

CHARMER: Des has the knack of
making people feel special.

(UNIVERSAL PICTORIAL PRESS)

ANNIVERSARY WALTZ: Des and partner Rose Diamond arriving
at the BBC's 60th anniversary bash.

(MIRROR SYNDICATION INTERNATIONAL)

HURT: Laura Ewing felt let down by Des when their passionate affair came to an acrimonious end. *(Above)*

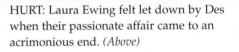

WHY DID HE DO THAT? Des co-presented the popular TV show *How Do They Do That?* with pretty Jenny Hull, but turned down a further series.

(ALL ACTION)

SPANISH AYES: Des and the BBC sports team at the 1992 Olympics in Barcelona.

(UNIVERSAL PICTORIAL PRESS)

LET'S BE FRANK: Des chums up with jockey Frankie Dettori at an awards bash.

(MIRROR SYNDICATION INTERNATIONAL)

PENSIVE: Des answers the questions for a change at a press conference to announce his defection to ITV in August 1999.

ON THE BALL: Des plays it for laughs after signing for ITV.

Des reacted with typical calm to the furore despite the fact that he was mortified by the publicity. 'While I will not go into any detail in my reaction,' he said, 'I will admit to an error of judgement which affects no one but myself and my long-term partner Rose.

'Rose has been aware of the situation for some months and has been both understanding and forgiving. Thankfully our fourteen-year relationship has, if anything, grown even stronger, despite a hiccup which many couples unhappily experience.'

A year after all the hullabaloo had died down, though, Laura Ewing was still bitter. The events had not just affected Des and Rose – they had affected Laura, too. Looking composed and immaculate in a charcoal grey trouser suit and silk blouse she recalled the excitement and passion of the affair but vowed:

'I wish it had never happened. It has turned my life upside down. My possessions are all in storage and I have got to go house hunting again. It's all a big mess.

'Des got what he wanted and when things became too hot, he got out of the kitchen. I was in love with him and he led me to believe that he loved me, too. I thought we had a future together but it all ended so badly.

'He used to call me his Scarlett O'Hara because of my red hair. But in the end he played the part of Rhett Butler. Frankly, he didn't give a damn.

'Des was a coward and a cad. We enjoyed some very nice times together but, in the end, he couldn't face me and tell me it was over. He just left me hanging on the end of a telephone line with the words "Never say never".

'Everyone has the right to change their minds if they don't want to be in a relationship, but if he had had the courage to come to me and say "This is not working" or, "It's not going to work. Let's call it a day, let's get rid of the home we had planned to share and sort out the financial consequences," then that would have been different. It would certainly have been the more mature thing to do.

'But to just ring me up and say, more or less, "The papers have been on to Rose and we will have to cool it for a while . . ." '

Laura was also furious at the way Des referred to their affair in his brief statement about it, calling their passionate time together an 'error of judgement'. Says Laura, 'It was a very self-ish thing for Des to have said. It was very dismissive of me and I resent being dismissed like that.'

Ironically, Laura and Des had just shared the best night of their time together when the alarm bells went off and the relationship started clattering rapidly towards the buffers. Laura had gone to Paris, at Des's request, by Eurostar train and checked into the hotel he had carefully selected for her, the £200-a-night Hotel de Buci, which was across the city from the Hotel de Louvre where the BBC squad was staying.

'That night in Paris was probably the most romantic of our time together,' says Laura.

'I had arrived on the Friday evening but Des was held up through work and said we'll make lunch tomorrow. We had a wonderful time. We had a long, liquid lunch together at a café called Les Deux Magots and then went back to the hotel. We made love in the afternoon but Des had to go and cover a football match at four o'clock until eight o'clock, and he eventually came back to me about nine.

'We sat in the hotel bar and ordered a bottle of cham-pagne, which Des put on my room bill. It was a nice hotel with a lovely piano bar but we were going out for dinner so we left half the bottle of champagne and got them to send the rest up to my room for later. I was so happy. The city was teeming with journalists but Des didn't seem to care. As usual he was very tactile. It was as though he didn't care who saw us. That was all part of the reason I believed him when he told me his relationship with Rose was all but over.

'He was the same in London. He would hold my hand

in the street and he took me for lunch to Bibendum and to Quaglino's and to a party at Richard Branson's house. He kissed me passionately in public and in taxis, and when we went house hunting, we did so together. He even picked me up in his Jaguar at the Langham Hilton opposite the BBC.

'But that morning, after he left me to go back to the BBC hotel, it all changed. He rang me about half past nine and said that he would not be able to see me again while he was in Paris because the Press were on to him. He did not seem worried, though. He was very calm about it, but he said it would be best if we did not meet because it would be embarrassing for the BBC if we had our photographs on the front page. So I said, I might as well go home then, which I did. Des had asked me to go to Paris and said he would pay for the trip but he never paid a penny.

'When I got home, he suggested I go away for a while and he would pick up the bill. Looking back I think he wanted to get me out of the way while the Press interest subsided, so I went to New York with a friend. But again he didn't give me a penny towards it.'

Laura could not have imagined the dramatic – perhaps traumatic – way things would turn out when she moved into an exclusive riverside development by the Thames at Chiswick in West London in December 1995. But she had an immediate effect on Des, who had moved into his £750,000 house with Rose a few months earlier. Laura, petite and pretty with a fabulous figure, was forty-seven and had been a widow for ten years. Her late husband had been a member of Lloyds and she had been left well provided for financially.

She recalls:

'Des hounded me from the moment I moved in. It was quite embarrassing really. I kept my distance as best I could – I thought he was married. Just a couple of days after I had moved in he jumped out of his car and ran across to introduce himself to me. I knew who he was but I was not in awe of him or anything and I didn't think anything about it.

'While we were chatting I must have mentioned that I was trying to sort out the curtains and that evening Rose came round. Des had sent her across with the name of a curtain maker. It was a nice neighbourly thing to do. After that we would chat whenever we saw each other over the next six months or so and I would see Des coming and going from my window. He would often look up and smile or wave.

'After that I sensed that Rose became a bit off with me. Des had told her that he thought I was attractive and maybe she sensed that something was wrong. Women are not stupid and Des was so obvious sometimes I felt very uneasy. Once Des was showing me a holiday brochure for a hotel in Ireland and I could see out of the corner of my eye, Rose looking daggers at me.'

Laura, like Des, is Irish. She came from a small town in County Laois. They had a rapport, but Laura was still trying to keep her distance.

The relationship changed in August 1997 after she called round at Des's to ask Rose for advice on the community tax which residents in the development were due to pay. Rose's Ford Ka was in the drive, but it was Des who answered the door.

'He was very theatrical saying, "Oh Laura, do come in . . . how lovely to see you," and all this. He insisted on pouring us a glass of wine each and then started to ask all sorts of personal questions: What did I do? Where did I go? I thought I had better leave. He was obviously chatting me up rather than just being friendly.

'Then when he found out I wasn't in a relationship any more he said, "What you need is a good Irishman." I said I didn't know any Irishmen at that time and suddenly he put his hand up in the air and said, "There's one here." I told him I had to go but he said we must have a drink sometime.

'I left and went home around the square but the next minute there was a knock at the door and it was Des. He said, "I'll have that other glass of wine now."

'He came in and said he was going through a really bad time, that it was finished between himself and Rose. I said, "Come on, don't be silly, everyone goes through bad stages." "No", he said. "It's really finished this time. We have had our ups and downs but it's finished." He said he and Rose hadn't had a physical relationship for three years.

'What do you say to something like that. I didn't know what to think. I found him attractive but he was in a long-term relationship and he lived next door to me. Over the next two weeks he started calling and asking me out to lunch but I refused.'

Then, after midnight on the night of Princess Diana's death, 31 August, Des called at Laura's home after he'd finished presenting *Match of the Day* and her resistance finally crumbled.

She says: 'We went upstairs to the lounge and he started kissing me. He kept saying he couldn't believe it was finally happening and that he'd dreamed of this moment for two years. He made me turn the light off and we sat in the dark drinking our wine and kissing. I felt my whole life was about to change. He said he had fallen out of love with Rose and in love with me. He said everyone needed a passion in their lives and I would be his.'

It was early the following week when they enjoyed their first lovers' lunch. Des had gone to his home on the Sussex coast with Rose but made the trip back to London by train to meet Laura. 'He took me to Bibendum and he was all over me in the restaurant,' she says.

'He wasn't hiding anything. Then he took me to Richard Branson's house for a party to launch his new cosmetics range and that's when I began to think, well, maybe he is serious about finishing his relationship with Rose. If he is going to be so blatant about it, to ask me out in public when the Press were there.

'So, I was taking him at face value. If he had tried to hide me or if I thought it was just a come-on line, an "Oh, my wife doesn't understand me" sort of thing, I might not have fallen so heavily for him and his charm. But we would have lunch in busy places, we would walk down the street together and he would be all over me in the restaurants. It was so public it was as though he didn't have anything to hide.'

The couple still had to tread warily close to home, however. They used to sneak away for early-morning rendezvous on their bicycles. Laura laughs at the memory: 'We both enjoyed cycling and we would meet around the corner from our homes at 7.30 in the morning. We would cycle along the riverbank.'

They were as happy as teenagers in love. 'It was heady stuff without a shadow of a doubt,' says Laura. 'There were plenty of nice lunches and champagne and a trip to Harrogate where Des was doing a business conference for Allied Domecq.

'At the Cadogan Hotel in Knightsbridge he would let his hands wander all over the place. As we were walking out it was the same. We were high on the emotion of it, enjoying every moment. The extra frisson of danger because it was slightly illicit and he had a partner just added to the excitement of it.'

But the pressures of keeping the affair from Rose were beginning to tell:

'One night, when we came back home from a night out he said, "Shall we go across and tell Rose about us?" I said it was for him to tell her and I didn't think I should be there when he did. He suggested things would be a lot easier if I moved, if I found a new home where we could both be together. He said, "I really want to get it right this time." He said neither of us had any money problems and we could get somewhere very nice together.

'He would give me cuttings from the newspapers about new developments – there was one over in Chelsea he wanted me to look at and another in the new Harrods Village near Barnes. Then he found this property in Marylebone, an area he knew well because he used to live there. In fact he sold his old place to Barbara Windsor and he took me round to see it. We went to look at the Marylebone mews house together and he felt it was just perfect. It had a garage for his Jaguar and it was close to the BBC. I took all that as a sign of serious intent. I was in love with him but he said that we were too close to Rose.'

Laura paid the deposit on the mews house and a quarter of the annual £34,000 rent herself, plus the costs of moving, decorating and furnishing the new home which she estimates at around £16,000. Des, who had promised to 'look after' her, transferred £10,000 to her bank from his account with Allied Irish in February 1998, and two further payments of £5,000 in May and June to help cover the rent.

But the storm clouds began to gather only days after they moved into the house on 23 February 1998. They spent just one passionate night there together before Des began to worry. Laura recalls:

'The Press were on to me from the first day I moved into the mews house. Someone knocked at my door to ask about Des but I had no intention of speaking to them. Then a letter came from a newspaper saying that they knew I was in a relationship with Des and did I want to talk about it. I didn't. I called Des and told him but he was very calm. He said, "As long as we don't say anything they have nothing to go on." Des was very sure of himself about that although, as a person, I would have to say he is a little insecure.

'He was also quite vain and he was very worried about losing his hair. He was afraid to comb it, he was that vain about it. When people recognized him he didn't mind most of the time. One time we were walking down Marylebone High Street when a traffic warden asked for his autograph. He quite liked that, but he said, "I expect you've given me a ticket." '

Laura laughs when she remembers the good times. But the bitterness of the break-up is never far away. She adds:

'It is not over for me. There's no way that I can move back to Chiswick now. I could not get over it when he suggested that I would have no problem in moving back there. Where I used to live I could not avoid seeing him and Rose. He is very self-centred. He is blinkered – thinking of himself all the time.

'He told me it would cost him £1.25 million to leave Rose and he has decided that is more important to him. I just wish he could have been more understanding and helped me with things. We both got into this but he left me to get out of it alone.'

How Des explained matters to Rose is anyone's guess, but his public reaction was a textbook example of how a high-profile public figure should handle a personal crisis. There were no unseemly skulkings, guilty face covered by a shading hand. No terse refusals to comment, or abuse aimed at those probing the open wound. He made a simple and dignified statement, calling his affair 'an error of judgement' and spent time behind closed doors with Rose as the whirlwind of publicity blew itself out.

Rose, a strikingly attractive blonde former model, professed that, of course, she still loved Des and added, 'We are still together. I have no intention of leaving him. I don't really want to talk about the affair. We have put it behind us.'

It seems clear that Des had confessed all some time before matters came to a head publicly. Whatever problems the couple had endured previously, how they were going to move forward in their relationship after his betrayal, were discussed privately if not always calmly. Des was not the first person to cheat on his partner and he won't be the last.

Former England rugby captain Will Carling was in the public spotlight at the same time over his affair with Lisa Cooke, wife of one of his playing colleagues. The public reaction to the two men could not have been more different. Whereas we were all willing to forgive Des, Carling was vilified. Clearly there was no sympathy for Carling because he and partner, Alison Cockayne, also had a baby boy to be considered. His attempts to explain his actions only made matters worse. As Des once remarked to Laura Ewing, 'If we don't say anything, they've got nothing to go on.' He was right.

In the aftermath of the affair, Des took Rose on holiday to Italy. They visited the Vatican and spent time in silent contemplation inside St Peter's Basilica. Whether Des was praying for forgiveness or thanking his lucky stars we do not know. But the couple spent a relaxed few days taking in the grandeur of the Eternal City – the majestic Colosseum, the romantic Trevi Fountain and the famous Spanish Steps. They wandered around the exclusive shops and enjoyed the delights of the many pavement cafés. Observers said Des was like a naughty puppy.

Until the unwanted headlines dragged their relationship into the limelight, Rosemary Diamond had managed to keep herself well away from the public side of Des's life. She grew up in Felixstowe and comes from an old Suffolk family. The daughter of an auctioneer and estate agent, she met Des at a party in London. After working as a model, Rose, who is six years younger than Des, became an interior designer and has turned both their London and Sussex homes into very stylish residences. Their relationship was for more than ten years the best-kept secret in television but she once confessed: 'Looking after Des is a full-time job.'

Rose's brother Robert Diamond, who works in the library of the *East Anglia Daily Times* in Norwich, says: 'We are a family that sticks together. We have always been a Suffolk family. I have had national newspapers asking me questions about Rose many times before but I never talk to them about my sister.' She was, however, said to be deeply upset when her parents' marriage ended in divorce.

In many ways Des is a victim of his own image as a ladies' man. For sure he prefers the company of women to men. Though he's happy and at ease in his sporting environment he's not really a pubby, clubby sort of bloke who wants to sink pints and laugh uproariously at inane jokes. In football terms he's not a back-of-the-terraces man, more a directors' box aficionado.

He admits to being a flirt and loves nothing better than chatting up the best-looking women at a party. He once said: 'I like women's company probably better than men's. I certainly hate those all-male dinners you sometimes have to go to. When a gang of men get together without female company they go back to prepubescent years. The wit goes out and the raucous stupidity comes in, and I'm not very good in that kind of company.

'Women give life balance and style and they give it some beauty. What's wrong with that?'

Over the years, Des has enjoyed the company of many beautiful women. It's only natural. Success is a big draw to women – they love successful men. Especially those who appear on television and have obviously got on very well in life. He is also good looking and extremely charismatic. Add to that the aura of social power and accomplishment which goes with the business of being on television and you've got the recipe for overwhelming success with women.

Psychologist Dr Glenn Wilson, Reader in Personality at the University of London Institute of Psychiatry, says:

'It is a characteristic of women that they flock around dominant men like insects drawn to the light. When men are successful or triumphant they get a surge in their own testosterone which primes them for sexual activity.

'Probably the origin of it can be seen in the case of when a couple of stags fight it out, the winner experiences a surge of testosterone and the loser a depression in its brain chemicals so that it goes away and doesn't bother any more. But the other guy is raring to go with the females – to take the trophy – and the same thing has been observed with male sportsmen.

'Successful men experience changes in their hormones and brain chemicals that makes them feel sexier. That, in turn, is perceived by the women and the whole thing is a positive spiral.'

If a red-blooded heterosexual male has any tendencies in that direction he is going to be faced with temptation frequently.

'A bit of the Bill Clinton effect is going to be apparent,' adds Dr Wilson.

'It is not an uncommon effect, in fact it is perfectly usual for powerful men – think of J.F. Kennedy, or Clinton, or film stars like Warren Beatty. Assuming that they are heterosexual to begin with and are attracted to women, then it's very hard for them to stop themselves. There is nothing pathological about it, it's normal human behaviour. The problem is that sometimes it can get a little messy for the people around you.

'The women involved with these types of men have to develop a degree of tolerance or a hard skin or whatever to accept the fact that they have got a red-blooded man who is at the peak of social power. He is going to have a lot of women who are out to share a bit of that with him.

'In a way they should see that as a positive thing. You can sometimes see the reverse of it. Women who would get upset if their own husband was having an affair or something can be derisory about a neighbour's husband who is such a wimp that no other woman would want him. Women see this as a two-edged sword.'

Des and Rose certainly managed to weather the storm that his affair with Laura Ewing created. By the end of 1998 they had been together for nearly fifteen years but friends began to wonder if, as a result of the affair, Des was finally going to marry his long-term partner. There is no sign of that. When his first marriage ended in bitter divorce Des was badly hurt. Perhaps he sees his long-term relationship with Rose as a form of marriage effectively, and doesn't feel the need to 'make it legal'. His Catholicism may also play a part – in that although his first wife divorced him, he sees the prospect of a second marriage as out of the question.

In common experience, though, it is probably true that the older you get the less likely you are to commit matrimony. Older bachelors do build an immunity to marriage and are often happiest in a solid, but less formal, relationship.

He was happily married to childhood sweetheart Susan Skinner in 1965 but their relationship broke down after Susan fell for another man while Des was busy chasing his career prospects up at the BBC in London. After his divorce in 1974 he set out to rebuild his life and enjoy the fruits of his career success. His name has been variously linked with newsreader Moira Stewart and former *EastEnders* actress Anita Dobson amongst others. Moira, a famously private individual, has always steadfastly refused to comment. But a spokeswoman for Anita Dobson says: 'I know this gets referred to from time to time but they have not had a romantic relationship. I think it all stemmed from Des saying he fancied her, or Anita saying that Des was dishy or something like that.'

It is one aspect of the fame game which causes continued annoyance to people like Des in particular. A rumour becomes a fact, a throwaway line or overheard remark becomes a story. And once in print, it continues in perpetuity.

But there is one relationship from this period which frequently comes back to haunt him. The summer of 1979 is one which Des Lynam will never be allowed to forget. It is a year he wishes had never happened. In fact, he may well look back on the twelve months which followed as his own personal 'annus horribilis', as the Queen once famously remarked after the negative publicity had exposed traumatic relationships within the Royal family.

For Des, it all began quite simply. There was a gorgeous girl, with flawless skin, sparkling green eyes and a sexy smile topping off a fabulous 37-25-37 figure. Quite naturally, the handsome television smoothy was instantly attracted. As, so he later pointed out, any normal man would have been.

Des had been divorced from his wife Susan for a good five years and he was happily enjoying the bachelor lifestyle and trappings of success which his flourishing career had brought him. And when he was introduced to a stunning model called Caroline Cossey at a flat in Kensington, West London, his natural inclination was to ask her out to dinner. It was the beginning of a relationship which has embarrassed and haunted him ever since.

Caroline had, in fact, been born a man. Twenty-five years before she was introduced to Desmond, she was born Barry Cossey in rural Norfolk and grew up as a boy. Aged seventeen, she moved to London and started living as a woman, finally succumbing to the forces which were tearing her apart – the agony of being a woman trapped in a man's body. In an era when society dismissed the issues of transsexuality as pure 'deviancy', Caroline found that she could satisfy her need to be a woman under the cloak of anonymity that big city life offered.

In 1974, after changing her name by deed poll, she finally had a sex change operation and, for the first time, felt as though she wasn't living a lie. Finally, she was a woman. As she herself recalls it: 'I had surgery to reconstruct my three-piece suite, as I like to call it. It was so successful that, since then, no man has been able to tell the difference between me and someone who was born a woman.'

So successful, indeed, was the transformation that for the next five years Caroline actually built up a successful modelling career, using the name Tula for her assignments. In 1981, just over eighteen months after meeting Des, she even appeared as one of the glamourpusses in the James Bond film *For Your Eyes Only*. And later she revealed her womanly charms for the magazine *Playboy*.

It was no wonder then, that, without any inkling of Caroline's past, Des was smitten when another model, called Cathy, took him to meet her. Caroline, too, was charmed by the old Lynam magic. She recalls: 'He was tall, dark and gorgeous, with the most beautiful thick dark hair, streaked with grey, and this beautiful moustache. I thought he was terribly handsome and attractive.'

Des, who was thirty-seven at the time, phoned Caroline a few days after their chance meeting and invited her to dinner. She says: 'I was thrilled. Des wasn't like any of the other men I'd known. He was more mature and successful. He exuded power. He was charming and intelligent. I found myself falling for him on that first date. We had a lovely night and I invited him back to my flat for coffee.

'At the end of the evening he pecked me on the cheek. I felt like he wanted more but he was a gentleman and he acted impeccably.'

The friendship progressed and Caroline says she was delighted when Des kissed her after dinner on their third date. She says: 'He was the most wonderful, passionate kisser. I loved the way his moustache tickled my face. He was very strong and his kisses were urgent, very sexy and seemed to last for ever. He was a very touchy-feely man. He liked to stroke my arm if we were in a restaurant and he would rest his hand on my leg in the car. He was very physical.'

Caroline insists that theirs became a full physical relationship before Des learned the truth about her sex change, but Des has always angrily fended off questions about the nature of his relationship with Tula. It's easy, I think, to understand why.

When Caroline married in 1992 in Montreal, Canada – where it is legal for a transsexual to marry a man – her husband, Canadian-born David Finch, revealed:

'These guys say to me: "You know ... what's it like ... down there?" I say to them: "Hey, I graduated in engineering not gynaecology."

'Another guy, a cop in Montreal, acted like a concerned friend when all he really wanted to do was to see my reaction when I spoke to him about it. He believed I was having a relationship with nothing more than a mutilated man. Our relationship was a good way of sorting out our true friends from those who couldn't accept us.

'Some of those I thought were my friends regarded me

as gay or thought that I must be confused, but fortunately I have always been very secure about my own sexuality. Actually what they were accusing me of was unfair to gay people, because if I was gay, I wouldn't be attracted to such a beautiful lady as Caroline.'

For someone in the public spotlight, like Des, the reaction to news that he had a 'transsexual girlfriend' would have been intolerable. By nature a person who tries to keep his personal life away from the Press, Des was torn between his feelings of friendship for Caroline – and sympathy with her situation once he learned the truth – and his natural desire not to be dragged into the middle of a sensational story.

He continued his friendship through 1980 and even met Caroline's mum Doreen. But Caroline noticed an immediate difference in his attitude when he learned that the stunning, blonde 6-foot model had actually been born a boy. She says: 'That night he looked me in the eye and said, "I know all about you. I don't want you to think you've got the last laugh on me."

'I felt like someone had just punched me in the tummy. I blurted out, "What are you talking about, who told you?" He just smirked and said, "Someone in the business." '

That wasn't the end of their friendship, though. They continued to meet but by the end of the year Caroline was afraid that her story was about to come out. Reporters had been nosing around in her home village, asking questions. She says: 'I warned Des about the risk and he said that he understood my fears. Even so I always sensed our relationship was fine while it was private. But I knew my past would come out and I didn't know if he would be there for me if it did.'

Her story was finally exposed by a Sunday newspaper in August 1981 – although Des's involvement was not. Caroline referred to her relationship with him in her autobiography, *My Story*, in 1991, but it wasn't until four years later that the episode made front page news in British tabloid newspapers.

Des was mortified by claims that theirs had been a passionate, physical affair and he retorted: 'It wasn't a sexual relationship that I can remember. But certainly, before I knew her situation, I found her very attractive, as any man would. But I don't remember making love.'

In private conversations, he has been heard to joke that he continued his usual habit of *not* asking to see a woman's birth certificate, but he is clearly embittered that this episode in his life should find particular fascination with the great British public. He says:

'I took her out on four or five dates. After that we had a distant friendship. I keep hearing her refer to her relationship with me as if it was something dramatically special and involved, but it didn't seem that way to me at the time. It wasn't the case. The number of times I met her could be counted on two hands.

'She would have forgotten about me years ago if I had been a bank manager but because I'm high profile she keeps referring to me. After I discovered her past it was clear the relationship was not going to go very far. Unless I was absolutely psychotic, I don't ever remember making love to her.'

A close friend of Caroline's says: 'She really is an amazing looking woman – from the tips of her manicured fingernails to her painted toenails. If she walked into a restaurant any man would turn his head and stare. She has been terribly hurt by the rejection she has received over the years but I think now she has learnt that not everyone can handle the kind of attention she naturally creates. She was very fond of Des and very hurt when he stopped calling.'

Her husband David Finch can also understand how Des might have felt. He recalls how it came as a bombshell when Caroline broke the news about her past by giving him her book, and telling him to go away and read it. He says:

'When I got it I was really shocked. I felt utter disbelief.

'I had lived the bachelor life and run around town but I can honestly say I had never been as fulfilled, both emotionally and sexually, as I was with her. But to read the book, I thought I had stepped into the Twilight Zone. I did not know about transsexuals and felt, rather ignorantly, that I had been fooled. I was angry. It was a reaction that is ignorant and one now that I am ashamed of.

'I read the book and learned from it. She could not help the way she was born, the chemical imbalance in her body and that, maybe, she was a woman after all.'

Some time after his friendship with Tula, but before he met Rose, Des had a serious relationship with a beautiful lady who is definitely all woman – the Scottish actress and singer Barbara Dickson. A former BBC executive told me: 'Oh, he was totally smitten with Barbara. We all thought this was the one, that the relationship would last. After his divorce Des had plenty of girl-friends. He's a good-looking guy, let's face it, and he enjoyed bachelor life to the full. But when he started going out with Barbara it was obviously something more than casual.

'When they eventually broke up he was devastated.'

Barbara, who has had a spectacularly successful career herself, winning awards as a singer and accolades for her part in the popular television drama *Band of Gold*, once confessed that she would rather have stayed single and childless than to have married a dangerous man. Considering Des's reputation I asked her if she had been referring to him when she said that. 'No,' she said categorically. She had been thinking of someone else, someone who was not famous or even involved in television but with whom she'd had a disastrous relationship before meeting and eventually marrying Oliver Cookson, a stage manager eleven years her junior.

She didn't wish to go into detail about her relationship with Des but she said:

'I never discuss any particular person I have been intimate with without their permission. But I was not talking about Des. He is a very nice man, a pleasure to know. I don't think that Des is dangerous in any sense but he is a lot more complex than people may think. Des is very uncommitted and I believe that people very, very rarely change.

'I think that leopards do not change their spots, regard-less of what people say. I think they just paint their spots the same colour as the rest of their fur – but the spots are still there. People who are prone to a certain pattern of behaviour are like that all their lives as long as they can get away with it. When they get older and say, "Oh I've grown up", they haven't really.'

6

Horses for Courses

'Des made an impassioned plea on behalf of the horse's manhood. We were so impressed that we voted to keep the horse intact.'

– Jame Lawless, racing syndicate member

Brilliant sunshine pouring out of a blue sky helped to make the last Grand National of the old millennium a sparkling occasion. As ever, Des Lynam was at the heart of one of the country's greatest sporting spectacles – one which, perhaps more than any other, appeals to all strands of the nation; the great and the good, the sporting and the non-sporting and, of course, the once-a-year punters for whom the National is a great British institution.

'We don't know what's going to win this year's race, do we yet,' he announced then added with a wink: 'Well, perhaps you do. I'm not so sure.'

It is no secret that in his many years of presenting the BBC's coverage of the event from Aintree, Des has grown into as much of a housewives' favourite as the big race itself. What not too many people outside the sport know is that Des has a great passion for racing and racing people. His enthusiasm for presenting what he calls 'one of sport's great days' is down to his own love of horse racing, as well as his natural joy at being part of one of the biggest events in the annual sporting calendar.

In his early days, living with his grandparents in Ennis, horses were a part of everyday life. His Uncle Frank, of course, was the last blacksmith in Ennis and young Desmond, who was the apple of everyone's eye, would grow to realize that horses were 'in his blood'.

His cosy chats with the legendary trainer Jenny Pitman have become one of the eagerly awaited highlights of the pre-race coverage, and on that warm April day of 1999 there was even greater anticipation than usual because it was due to be Pitman's last appearance at the event as a trainer.

Des cheerfully trailed his by now customary chat with Jenny, known to one and all as 'the cuddly one', by introducing a visit he had made to her yard at Lambourn in Berkshire, home of Nathan Lad, her current hope, and of the former National winners she had saddled, Corbiere and Royal Athlete. While touring the stables earlier in Grand National week, he also made a visit to the stall of the great Garrison Savannah, which won the Gold Cup at Cheltenham for Pitman, but narrowly failed in a bid to pull off an extraordinary double by winning the National as well.

It was heartwarming stuff. Two people with more than just an excellent working rapport and a genuine love of horses talking about good times past.

But for many people watching at home, the predominant image of Des and Jenny Pitman will always be from a much more dramatic and painful occasion – from the year when the Grand National had to be abandoned after bomb threats from the IRA. The sight of Jenny Pitman in tears as she told Des of her anguish at having to leave behind the horses she so clearly loves; when no one knew if or where a bomb, or bombs, had been placed by the terrorists; was one of the saddest and most enduring records of the event down the years.

The outrage made it the most extraordinary Grand National ever – stranger even than the National that never was, when two false starts meant the race was abandoned; and more memorable, for all the wrong reasons, than the incredible epic of 1967 when a rank outsider, Foinavon, crossed the finish line first after virtually every other horse had fallen in an amazing pile-up or had been pulled up at other fences. That was probably *the* race which assured us all that, well, in this life we've *all* got a chance . . .

The day the IRA wrecked the Grand National was 5 April 1997. It was also the day which proved that Des was the man for all seasons; that when the manure hit the fan, Des wouldn't let you down. In television presenting there is nothing more precarious than hosting a live event. Nervous producers go through hell when a technical hitch threatens to disrupt the smooth running of their programme. If the front man lets you down, then you're sunk.

Des had, and has only enhanced, a reputation as a man who could handle a crisis. He has developed a fatalistic approach which allows him to take the viewer into his confidence. There's a problem, let the viewer know. If the satellite link has gone down, or there's some other insurmountable event, tell the people watching why you are having to fill the airtime with flannel. On one occasion at Wimbledon, when yet another downpour had left him virtually bereft of things to talk about, he famously interviewed his dog.

When Sir Cliff Richard stood up in his seat to entertain a restless Centre Court crowd, Des quipped: 'I hope he doesn't do "Summer Holiday".' He did.

But on the scale of problems they don't come much bigger than an entire event being closed down midway by a bomb scare, and some other presenters, you may feel, might have gone blank with panic.

Another enduring image of that event was of the managing director of Aintree, Charles Barnett, announcing to Des and the cameras: 'I would like to ask everybody – and that includes you from the BBC – to leave the course and get out on to the public highway immediately.'

Coolly, Des replied: 'Thank you Charles, we will do that almost immediately. Just to say, at home, I am afraid to say the Grand National of 1997 has been ruined.' Des, who had been describing the pandemonium and trying to interview course officials about the threat, then continued to bring to the viewers the images of bewilderment, including his famous interview with Pitman.

The 1997 National, which was the one hundred and fiftieth, was also to be the last one for the veteran commentator Peter

O'Sullevan, who had been calling the horses around Aintree for fifty years. He was honoured with the unveiling of a bronze statue of himself by Princess Anne, but was then caught up in the mêlée as up to 70,000 racegoers attempted to leave the course.

The bomb warnings had been received at 2.49 pm by a telephonist at Liverpool's Fazakerley Hospital and an authenticated IRA codeword was given. A second call had been given three minutes later to the police control centre in Marsh Lane, Bootle. Immediately, the massive evacuation plan swung into action. The warnings had claimed that a bomb would go off at 3.50 pm when crowds would have been thronging the stands to watch the thirty-eight horses and riders compete around Aintree's infamous 4.5-mile course.

Apart from the concern for people's safety, the evacuation calls proved frustrating for broadcasters like Des and Sir Peter O'Sullevan, as he now is. The amazing scenes as police on horseback shepherded people away from the Canal Turn fence where the callers said a device had been planted, and emptied the enclosures, bars and restaurants was, obviously, a major news event which they wanted to broadcast live to the stunned viewers at home. The event, after all, attracts a worldwide viewing figure in excess of 400 million – and what riveting viewing it was in the unfolding drama. But the warnings were clear and uncompromising. Everyone out. And that included the BBC.

Sir Peter later recalled being told to leave and he replied: 'That's ridiculous. If people have been told to clear the course, I have to describe that.'

As coverage from Aintree was closed down, the BBC ran a documentary about the legendary footballer, Pelé, to fill in the time. In the meantime racegoers, unable even to get their cars from the car parks, flooded into Liverpool where a wartime spirit saw strangers sharing makeshift accommodation and singsongs. Even the jockeys were stranded in their racing silks, wandering around the city looking for places to stay.

Three suspect packages were eventually detonated in controlled explosions, but they turned out to have been harmless. The entire nation had been hoaxed.

In the uproar which followed there were universal calls from racegoers, jockeys, owners and trainers for the National to be run within days of the hoax, rather than allow it to be abandoned. There was more than £70 million riding on the outcome, after all. Incredibly it was run forty-eight hours later and more than 20,000 people gathered on that bleak Monday to watch the one-race event despite a further threat from the would-be bombers. The Grand National of 1997 finally went ahead at 5.00 pm on Monday, 7 April, as the only race on the card. A unique event.

When it was all over, the course emptied in less time than it had taken Lord Gyllene, a generously priced 14-1 shot, to romp to victory by 25 lengths. Pretty soon, amongst the empty beer cans and general race-day debris, all that remained was, once again, Des Lynam, leaning against the rails doing his pieces to camera for the replays and re-runs.

It was a triumph for the organizers and a triumph for the authorities and everyone who attended – not least the journalists and television crews. There had, in fact, been twenty-five determined bomb calls since the event had initially been postponed, but the security forces decided to call the IRA's bluff and the event went ahead. Fortunately most of the 20,000 racegoers present were unaware of the latest series of threats. Some had come from cranks and obvious hoaxers. But some had chillingly borne the IRA codeword.

Some in that brave crowd must have harboured dark thoughts in the recesses of their minds. Des Lynam might even have considered that the outrage of two days earlier had been the first bomb alert to affect a national event since the bombing in his hometown of Brighton disrupted the Conservative Party Conference.

Amidst widespread condemnation of the terrorist action, Charles Barnett, managing director of the course, paid tribute to everyone who stood firm and ensured the race was finally run, saying: 'There was a great swell of feeling in the racing industry that it had to go on. The Grand National is a hugely important sporting event – one of the ten most important in the world.'

Racing legend Sir Peter O'Sullevan says:

'Des handled his aspect of that drama just as immaculately as one would expect. I have known Des both profession-ally and socially for a while and I am a keen admirer. His great characteristic is so well known – he is so exception-ally composed, which is something I have always admired. He does his homework so that he's as familiar as he can be with the setup before the Grand National and those sorts of events where I have been associated with him.'

Clearly that was the most nerve-wracking Grand National in history, but there have certainly been others which were extra-ordinary in their own way. Des says: 'We have been covering the Grand National on live television at the BBC for some forty years. We first broadcast it in 1960 with sixteen cameras provid-ing revolutionary coverage. That race was won by Merriman.'

He recalls clearly the punters' favourite race of 1967 when Foinavon romped home, and the introduction of colour trans-mission to the coverage in 1969. At that time Des was just begin-ning his career with Radio Brighton, but how he envied the BBCs top presenter of the day, David Coleman, who brought the big event into homes across the country.

The 1970s were the Red Rum years – one of those great horses which the nation takes to their hearts. Red Rum won the National three times and notched up two seconds to claim his place as the greatest National horse of all time.

Probably the biggest fiasco in Grand National history occurred in 1993 when two false starts led to the event which was dubbed the 'National That Never Was'. It was a disaster all round – for the punters, for the jockeys, for the trainers and even for the bookies. For one man, however, it was an unmiti-gated triumph. Des was once again centre stage as the roof caved in, as it were, on this major sporting spectacle. And, once again, his cool nerve in the face of a dramatic turn of events proved to be the BBC's trump card.

Punters both at home and on the course were disappointed when starter Captain Keith Brown lined up the horses for the cavalry charge to the first fence, only to signal a false start because some horses had bolted into the tape. With excitement mounting, the horses and riders reassembled behind the tape and as Captain Brown's flag came down they lurched forward once again. Incredibly, some horses got caught in the tape again, but the majority got away and headed down the course. Another false start was signalled and all hell broke loose.

Some riders were frantically waved down before the first fence; others didn't realize a false start had been called and galloped off on the first circuit. All in all it was a catastrophe.

In the days of the inquest which followed, Des Lynam and the BBC outside broadcast team were singled out for praise for the way in which they quickly established what was going on and relayed the facts, the anguish and the bitter disappointment of everyone closely involved back to the viewers at home.

TV personality Esther Rantzen, writing in the *Daily Express*, asked:

'Wasn't the Grand National That Never Was the most brilliant piece of live television coverage you have ever been gripped by? From the moment the tape broke, a hovering aerial camera showed us exactly what happened as the fluttering ribbon caught round a jockey's neck and trailed across the course like the thin curling wave at the prow of a speedboat.

'From then on, the place to be was watching BBC1. That team did not miss a shot, or an interview. Desmond Lynam held it together with interviews that vividly expressed the rage and disbelief of riders and trainers.

'If we had been at Aintree we would have seen so little by comparison, just chaos and confusion. But thanks to that amazing outside broadcast team we saw and heard everything.'

If Des was the only winner of the race that never was, he decided to have a crack at becoming a winner in the real event the following year by saddling a horse and joining the other proud owners as part of the great day rather than just the man who brings it into millions of homes. His enthusiasm for the task had been fuelled some years earlier, in 1986, when he leased a horse for the Grand National and thoroughly enjoyed the thrill of being so personally involved.

The horse was a thirteen-year-old called Another Duke, and although it had top jockey Paul Nichols on board and was trained by the legendary Josh Gifford, the bookies probably rated its chances accurately by offering odds of 200-1. The dream, however, was not to be fulfilled in '86. Another Duke ran gamely despite a blunder at the notorious Becher's Brook on the first circuit and carried on for three more fences before succumbing to the inevitable at Valentine's.

But it was enough to hook Des. He says: 'Despite being an outsider the whole thing really grabbed me, and although he made that monumental blunder at Becher's Brook on the first circuit, he survived for three more fences. It's a terrific thrill to be a part of the Grand National.'

His interest aroused, Des enlisted the help of his friend and fellow broadcaster Julian Wilson to find a horse which he could buy, put into training and enjoy as an owner rather than merely 'renting' a horse for the event. It may surprise a lot of people to learn that you can lease a horse, which is already in training, for an event like the Grand National but it is fairly common practice.

Anyway, buoyed by Des's enthusiasm and optimism, Wilson set about the task of finding him a horse. He recalls:

'Des had always talked broadly about an interest in having a racehorse or a share in one and I thought it was something he should do.

'I said to him, "Let's go to Ireland and I'll find you a proper racehorse and you can have some fun." I flew him out to Shannon and we went to visit the stables of Tom Costello at Newmarket on Fergus in County Ennis. I thought it was a fortunate meeting. After all, Des is Irish and I knew he came from that part of the world. It turned out that Des's uncle had been a farrier in Ennis and he had shod the Costello horses for years. There was a great rapport between the two great men.

'We looked at a couple of horses, one by Remainder Man

and another which had good credentials. We liked them both but in the end I persuaded Des to buy the one by Remainder Man. It was a lovely four-year-old that would have been ready to run in about three months and I'm sure that after a little work with Josh Gifford the horse would have proved good value for the asking price of around £25,000.

'Anyway once he got home and back into the loving arms of Rose, Des seemed to have a change of heart. He said she had talked him out of it and he had decided that yes, it would all become a little bit expensive.

'Des is generous of spirit but I think he was a little bit worried that the horse might mean an examination of how deep his pockets were. It put me in mind of that great Eric Morecambe gag: "I'm wearing my BBC suit today – you know, small cheques." Des simply decided it was too expensive a project.'

So, the Grand National of 1994 began without a horse owned by Mr Desmond Michael Lynam, trained by Josh Gifford and ridden by whoever . . . But, if he didn't have a horse in the race, he had the next best thing – a horse owned by his friend, the comedian Freddie Starr.

Thousands of punters were thrilled and delighted when Miinnehoma (correct with two i's) owned by the flamboyant Starr romped home in the world's greatest steeplechase. It was a race and a result, everyone agreed, to restore the reputation of the event after the fiasco of the previous year. This time the only people left complaining were the bookies who caught a cold as people took a late flutter on the horse which was trained by the champion trainer Martin Pipe and ridden by the champion jockey Richard Dunwoody but had been offered at very reason-able odds of 16-1.

In extremely testing conditions of cloying mud and the most difficult fences in world racing, only six horses out of the thirty-six starters managed to finish. At the final fence, the favourite Moorcroft Boy was in the lead but after the horse faltered, it was down to Miinnehoma and another little fancied horse, Just So.

The crowd went wild with delight as Miinnehoma held on to win by one and a quarter lengths and grab the £115,000 prize money for the comedian Starr.

No one was more delighted than Starr, who was not able to be at Aintree himself due to work commitments, but he had even more reason to celebrate than the sizable first prize cheque. Starr had also secretly put £10,000 on Miinehoma at odds of 33-1 which had been offered weeks before the race, and stood to collect another £330,000 from the bookies.

Viewers at home were treated to the delight of trainer Pipe and jockey Dunwoody, but what of the owner? Suddenly Des, who was as usual presenting live from the course, took a phone call from Starr himself. At home we could only guess what was being said as the unpredictable millionaire chuckled and roared away down the line to Des, who hummed and nodded and smiled and raised his eyebrows a time or two as he shared in private amusement with one of the country's best-loved comics. It was a surreal moment and another dazzling display of cool by the consummate link-man who won't be fazed by anything – not even Britain's most zany and unpredictable comic talent at the height of his Grand National winning ecstasy.

Later Starr revealed:

'Winning the Grand National is better than marriage and even better than sex. It's like an orgasm – only better. We watched the race at home and we all started off about ten feet away from the TV set. Then as the race went on we got nearer and nearer the screen, shouting Miinie home. By the finish, I was practically inside the television, so I thought I'd speak to Des. Actually I got a call from the trainer Martin Pipe and I said, "Where are you?" "In the winners' enclosure," he replied. I think that's when I spoke to Des. I was so excited I can't remember what I was going on about.'

Des's own dreams of joining the exclusive racehorse-owning set did not end with his decision not to go ahead with the purchase of the horse Julian Wilson had picked out for him, however.

Another, less costly, way to become an owner is to join a syndicate. You get the pleasure of owning a horse without the pain of having to foot all the bills yourself. Wilson, who has been involved in racing for many years, wished Des had called upon his experience before plunging in.

He says:

'Unfortunately he then got involved in a horse through a drinking club in West London, called Motcombs Club. The owners, who are very nice folk, gathered a few of their favourite customers together for a bit of a champagne session and then sold them each a one-twelfth share in a yearling bred by Pat Eddery.

'In the full flush of champagne they each parted company with £2,000 for a share in this beast. I am afraid it really was a dog-meat job. It had no distance, no resolution – nothing to recommend it at all. But in any event, they had a lot of fun with it.

'I had hoped that Des would have invested in something with even the remotest little bit of talent, though, than the horse which ran as Motcombs Club.

'Des just enjoys the social side of racing. It's funny for a man with a heritage from the south-west of Ireland not to have an interest in following the sport in greater detail. His friend John Motson is quite a keen student of racing. He knows what to look for and takes a great interest in the more detailed aspects.'

Wilson has known Des since his early days at the BBC and adds: 'There are only two sports Des doesn't really know a great deal about and they are the two he did his first broadcasts for the BBC about – racing and cricket. It was very nearly goodbye and thank you after his first broadcast for the BBC which was a cricket match. I am not sure he knew how many balls were in an over . . .'

Top trainer Neville Callaghan who took on the job of preparing Motcombs Club for racing at his stables in Newmarket wasn't quite as scathing as Wilson about the horse's qualities, but even he had to confess that it was not blessed with any great abundance of natural talent. 'I did train him for a while,' he recalls, 'but he wasn't very good. I met Des once or twice and he always seemed a nice, affable chap who enjoyed the atmosphere and being around the horses but he wasn't overly interested in the day-to-day stuff.'

Des's interest – and probably his vivid imagination – was most definitely fired up when the syndicate members met to discuss what to do about their under-performing beast. It is common knowledge in racing circles that a male horse may well improve its performance if a certain delicate operation is undertaken. Without going into unnecessary detail, the horse becomes a gelding. Many men would wince at the thought of a simple vasectomy, but Des was clearly horrified at the prospect of Motcombs Club becoming a gelding.

Jane Lawless, wife of the club and restaurant owner Philip Lawless, says: 'When our horse wasn't doing well we were told that gelding improves performance and were just about to vote for it when Des made an impassioned speech on behalf of the horse's manhood. He saved the day for Motcombs Club. We were so impressed that we voted to keep the horse intact.'

Trainer Callaghan says: 'When you are not into horses you might think gelding is a harsh thing to do to a horse, but it isn't really. It's true that gelding can improve the performance of some horses and that would have been my recommendation for Motcombs Club, but the owners decided against it.

'He was eventually sold on. Still, we got him racing and the owners enjoyed their days out.'

Des subsequently joined a syndicate with his good friend, the commentator John Motson, to take a one-tenth share in a horse called Out of the Deep. At least with Mottie and head of the syndicate David Ladhams, he was amongst a group of individuals whose expertise in the field surely exceeds Des's own. Out of the Deep, not out of your depth, eh Des? I remember meeting Mottie at Cheltenham in 1997 and over lunch with his friend Ricky George, he advised me to put some early money on Earth Summit for the Grand National later that year.

Ricky George was the owner and they confidently expected

the horse to do well. It did better than that, romping home for a sensational win. Unfortunately for me I'd forgotten all about Earth Summit until a couple of days before the National, then a sudden business trip to Brussels meant I didn't back anything at all in the race. The 'connections' had been able to get odds of better than 25-1 by backing early.

Out of the Deep went into training with Jim Old at his racing stables near Marlborough. He said: 'It is an unraced horse at the moment but eventually it will make up into a nice chaser, I hope.

'It's too soon to say if he'll be good but he's bred the right way, he looks the right way. We haven't done enough serious work with him to know whether he is or he isn't yet.'

The beauty of racing syndicates, says Old, is that:

'a lot of good friends can have a shared interest, a shared pain and a shared pleasure – and they can have get-togethers; they can come to see the horse and talk about it and look forward to it running. Maybe it will turn out to be a star and if it doesn't turn out to be a star then there's the post mortems and drinks to quell the pain of that, you know. It's just fun.

'Out of the Deep is not an expensive horse. It didn't cost an arm and a leg and nobody is going to go skint on it. It's much more of a social type thing than any serious pretensions that it's going to be a world beater or anything like that.'

I'm sure we will see Des picking up the silverware in the winners' enclosure yet.

Over the years Des has become an integral part of events from Aintree but Susie Hughes, widow of a former clerk of the course John Hughes, remembers when he first began covering the race and was almost overawed by the scale of the event. If you haven't been to a major meeting like the National or Cheltenham, it's hard to imagine the sheer logistical difficulties of nipping around from one part of the course to another – even if that just means getting from the parade ring to the winners' enclosure. Unlike a big crowd at, say, a football match, the crowds at race meetings are forever on the move. There's always something new to do – get a pre-race look at the horse you fancy, move into the grandstand, place your bet, buy a drink . . . It's like being just one ice cube in the constantly shifting ice pack but trying to determine your individual direction.

It all makes the job of anchoring a broadcast from the heart of an event just that little bit more difficult.

Susie Hughes recalls: 'My husband John was clerk when Des arrived for his first broadcast from Aintree and I think John helped him out a little bit. Des was the new boy after David Coleman, and quite a nervous one too. But he soon got the technique of how to get it right at Aintree and I think he has thoroughly enjoyed his years there. We had Des and Jimmy Hill over for dinner one evening and we had a very pleasant time.'

Julian Wilson remembers Des's first Aintree, too. He recalls:

'When Des first came over to television, some of those already there took up a bit of a defensive position. When he appeared a little uncomfortable doing cricket – which is not one of his sports, I mean he grew up in the south-west of Ireland – they used that and said, "Look, he's a radio man."

'In the spring of 1978 I had been discussing plans for Aintree with Alan Hart who was head of BBC Sport at that time and he was looking for somebody to present the first two days of the meeting. Coleman had come into the studio for *Grandstand* and wasn't doing outside broadcasts. I suggested Des and Alan wasn't sure, but I said he'd be fine and it was agreed. I knew racing was probably the only other major sport Des wasn't fully on top of, but we talked it through and he came up and presented the two days from Aintree during the week and Frank Bough did the Grand National on the Saturday. Des was fine, as cool and professional as you'd expect and the rest as they say is history.'

Clerk of the course Hughes had been instrumental in the Grand

National being saved in 1975 when there were plans to scrap the world-famous race. And when he died in 1988 the Aintree officials dedicated a race in his memory, which became known as the John Hughes Chase, previously the Topham Trophy. However, when, in recent years, rumours surfaced that the John Hughes Chase was going to be axed, those who knew him, including Des, were prepared to mount a vigorous campaign to save the race – just as John had saved the National itself.

But Susie adds: 'Aintree changed their minds but Des was more than willing to back us in our pleas that John's race should not be dropped. I got to know Des a little better after he and Jimmy Hill came to dinner. With the best will in the world, Des can get a little pompous at times, but I can still go up behind him and say, "Oi," and he will look round, from a great height – he's quite a big chap – and smile that lovely smile and say, "Oh, hello there. How lovely to see you." '

Lovely indeed.

Another side to Des that he likes to keep quiet about is his work for various charities. Through his love of racing he has always been keen to support the work in aid of the Spinal Injuries Association – a charity close to the heart of those who daily risk their bodies training and racing horses all over the country. Malcolm Palmer, of bookmakers Coral, says: 'For a number of years Des attended and then kindly acted as master of ceremonies at our ball in aid of the Spinal Injuries Association. It was a splendid occasion with more than four hundred guests at the Dorchester in London. Des was always very amusing and used to quite enjoy himself.'

Racing legend Sir Peter O'Sullevan recalls an occasion which both he and Des truly relished. It was a trip to the Cognac region of France with Grand National sponsors Martell. Sir Peter says:

'We had great fun, I remember, when we went with Martell and we flew to Cognac in a private jet to view the Martell operation and to see the distillation of cognac from the beginning. Both Des and I were extremely impressed with the cooperage. We thought this was almost the most fascinating aspect of the whole operation – how these guys made those wooden barrels in the real old style. We were both deeply impressed with that.

'Anyway, on the way back, we played a slight prank on our colleagues. We were in a private executive jet and Des went up the front to chat with the pilot during the return journey. He came back and claimed to have had a session in the cockpit flying the plane and he suggested that I went up and had a flying session with the pilot as well.

'I persuaded the pilot to just duck a little bit to the right, you know, to make the plane swing a little, which he did. I was only sitting beside him, just as Des had been. But Des told his BBC colleagues, "I knew Peter was going to insist on flying the plane. I'm sure he'll get the hang of it soon." We certainly worried our colleagues a little on that occasion.

'He's great fun, Des. He loves a bit of fun and he carries everything off absolutely marvellously.'

Sir Peter found himself on the receiving end of one of Des's little jokes when he turned up at an awards ceremony with his wife. Sir Peter says:

'I got some unexpected awards, purely for having lived so long, from a television society. Des and I kept meeting at these dinners because, by way of ensuring that I never returned to commentary, they kept making certain of it by giving me awards.

'The last time, my wife was there too – she doesn't usually come along to these things – and Des said to her, "I'm so glad that Peter has received an award . . . because it's been at least a week since he's had one." We have had quite a bit of fun together over the years.'

The feelings are mutual. Sir Peter is top of Des's list of broadcasting heroes. 'You try finding your own horse among thirty runners over six furlongs,' says Des. 'You don't spot it until after the race is over, but Peter had to name them all – and he did so into his eightieth year. He was also blessed with the greatest voice in sports broadcasting. When you get excited you shouldn't raise the pitch of your voice, you should bring it down. Some famous names who are still around have never realized that. Peter knew instinctively to lower his voice when something dramatic happened.'

7

Simply the Best

'What people see is just the tip of the iceberg when they see him perform. There's years of experience and hours of thinking going into each broadcast.'

– Brian Barwick, Head of ITV Sport

The tributes to Des's skill and professionalism which mean the most come from those who have worked closely with him. The former England manager Terry Venables, for instance, has worked with Des on many major football nights both during and after his reign as coach of the England soccer team.

'There's no one better,' says Terry, or El Tel as the British sporting public liked to call him after his stint as manager of Barcelona in Spain. 'I don't think there has ever been anyone better. He has been so outstanding for such a long period of time I doubt if anyone will equal him in the future either. He is that outstanding.'

The former head of the national team knows how much the professionals of the game enjoy their own sports coverage, which just emphasizes the point made frequently that if you don't know your stuff when you are in a position like Des's, you will soon be found out. Terry adds: 'England players would watch *Match of the Day* when we were together on international duty and they would discuss the football rather than the presentation or the opinions of the panel. But I think it's a foregone conclusion what their feelings are about Des – that he's the best at what he does.'

Terry also finally settles one of the most frequently asked questions about his appearances on BBC soccer panels. Just how did he get on with Jimmy Hill?

'We would always have a joke, Des and I, on those programmes and there were, of course, always arguments between me and Jimmy Hill. Des and I would be doing our Jimmy Hill impressions, which he knew about, but Des was the best at that as well.

'We would always tell Jimmy Hill stories. Just the mention of Jimmy's name always brings a smile to my face, and I mean that in the best possible way as well.

'Me and Jim got on famously. I know everyone didn't think that we did because we argued on screen. It wasn't an act, we did used to disagree a lot. I just thought that Jimmy was so positive that you would either agree or disagree – sometimes strongly. That would always make for good chat and cross examination.

'But off air we got on very well. I think that used to disappoint everyone.

'I remember cab drivers used to say, "You hate that Jimmy Hill, don't you?" And I'd say, "No, I don't." They'd say, "Go on, you do." So I'd say, "Oh, OK, I do." Then they'd go, "Yeah, I knew you did."

'I would tell Des things like this that would happen from time to time and then we would go off and chat to one another in our Jimmy Hill voices. It was a laugh.

'I actually took off Jimmy on his *This Is Your Life* show and he thought it was very funny. All the boys had a laugh on the panel. It's part of what makes it all work so well.

'Des just makes you so relaxed. You know some people put you on edge and that is their own nerves. Because he hasn't got any, Des immediately puts you at ease and that's very important for you.'

When Des first moved into television, Bob Wilson was already an integral part of the BBC sports team. Like everyone else, he quickly took to the new fella and he has watched – sometimes with awe, sometimes with frustration – ever since as Des has built a fantastic career which has even eclipsed that of the 'big two' of the time, Coleman and Bough.

A great friend, but also an earnest rival over the years, Wilson says:

'Des is unique in his style amongst broadcasters but there is another side to it as well. It doesn't guarantee you a successful programme having Des Lynam on it. It helps, but you've got to have a really good product as well. Des, when he did *How Do They Do That?*, did not get good figures, so what you must have is a good product.

'It is a cut-throat business. It's all about ratings and, more importantly these days, market share – what percentage of the audience tuned in.'

Wilson spent more than twenty happy years at the BBC, but eventually felt compelled to leave for ITV because, while at the Beeb, there was never any doubt that Des was top dog and Bob Wilson was Number Two. He says ruefully:

'When I had to make the decision about leaving the BBC for ITV the BBC said, "Well, come on, what do you want to stay?" My wife, who is also my agent, went into the negotiations and she was shocked. She saw everything that they were going to give me financially, which was just amazing. That was flattering. But what my wife could not understand is that I have always wanted to be Number One at whatever I do and while Des was there, there was no way I was going to be Number One.

'Now I understand the head of sport's problem. He would say there is only one chair, and I can see that, but it didn't help me. So when they said, "OK, if it's not about finances what will it take for you to stay?" I said, "Give me *Match of the Day*." Because I know that *Match of the Day* is a national institution. Even though the Beeb are losing all sorts of contracts on the sporting front, *Match of the Day* is still watched by five or six million football fans. It's nothing like it used to be but it's still a fantastic product.

'I knew what I wanted. I was still prepared not to be doing the World Cup Final and the FA Cup Final, which have come over to ITV since then, but I needed a bigger share. I did not just want to be the Number Two who did half the World Cup tournament but not the important half, the vital matches.'

It was clearly painful for an old sporting pro, full of competitive edge, to feel undervalued, especially in the one area where his knowledge was greatest. In football.

Wilson adds:

'It was a hell of a difficult time. I have never had a bad word to say about Des and I never will do because he is unique in his way. But they came back and made me a big offer on *Match of the Day* – that I would have a certain proportion, but the crunch question came when I said, "Well, who'll be presenting the World Cup Final, who will be presenting the European Championship Final." And of course I knew the answer. So in the end, it wasn't a difficult decision. I went to ITV in 1994.'

Ironically, after five years as the Number One football man at ITV, Wilson will again have to share centre-stage with Des at ITV.

In his early days, Wilson was the presenter of *Match of the Day*, along with Jimmy Hill. But, just as he displaced Coleman and Bough, Des would eventually find his way into the hot seat of the football fans' favourite show of the week. Over the years Des has earned a reputation as somebody who will not suffer fools gladly but also, some would say, as a man of intense ambition who would make a determined foe.

Wilson says:

'What is fascinating for me is that at the time Des arrived at the Beeb, David Coleman was really still kingpin on

Grandstand. Des began to do alternate Saturdays and I was working alongside both of them presenting *Football Focus*. Sometimes Frank Bough would be in the chair, too, until eventually Des more or less forced their hand, saying either this is my seat or it isn't.

'They had a big decision to make. Coleman is one of my heroes. He was a far greater broadcaster than anyone has ever given him credit for. He was of the time when there were none of the safety nets we have these days. His was a wing-and-a-prayer job. You've got to admire him.

'It was right-off-the-top-of-the-head stuff for five and half hours. *Grandstand* in those days was incredible, but Des did it too. In fact, he did it brilliantly. Having to keep your facts and figures up to date, particularly in that frantic last half an hour when all the games were coming in, which Coleman always did brilliantly, is no easy task. Steve Ryder does it excellently now.

'Eventually though, Des, obviously, had had enough of that and then it was on to other things and he replaced Jimmy Hill on *Match of the Day*. Jimmy was presenting *Match of the Day* with me doing some of the round-ups and presenting some of the *Match of the Day*s as well, but it eventually became Des's chair and still remains Des's chair.'

There have often been unfair and unflattering comparisons between Bob Wilson and Des Lynam, but recalling his own start in TV, Wilson says:

'I loved doing interviews. I'm not saying I did them very well. On one early one I repeated myself about twelve or thirteen times with one word, but I obviously created an impression because two or three days later the BBC got me on and two or three days after that I did *Sportsnight* with Frank Bough on an England game. Then they asked me to do part of the 1970 World Cup finals and I have done every World Cup since then.

'I finished playing football for Arsenal in 1974 and went

straight in with the BBC. I literally went straight in there and all credit to the BBC. If they hadn't had the patience it might have all been different. If you ask anybody who remembers me to begin with . . .

'There I was being so comfortable being interviewed, but as the presenter myself, with earpieces barking instructions at you and everything else you have to co-ordinate, it was a nightmare. At first I was just a block of wood. It isn't easy to present. People don't realize the complications there can be.'

But despite any friendly rivalry that exists between them, Bob is anxious to make it clear that as far as Des is concerned there was never any sense of triumphalism or 'I'm top dog and you are Number Two.' In fact, Des has often shown a generosity of spirit never better illustrated than when Wilson's own perceived limitations boiled over in frustration.

He says:

'Des has won awards all through his career for his style and the way he writes. There is one particular instance about Des, and it's the one time that I always say to people that he helped me to carry on. I am not saying that I was about to pack it in, but it used to frustrate me that he would have this way of delivering a line, often with a great deal of style and humour.

'But one day, it was one of the Olympic Games when I was doing the daytime session and Des was doing, as always, the primetime session. I remember going and picking up Des's script and I went, "Oh jeez, I wish I could find words like that."

'The difference is that while I'm a physical education teacher and a quite well-educated guy, with a background from Loughborough University, Des is a professional journalist and he's got a lovely little turn of phrase and a lovely sense of humour. He writes his own scripts and he ad-libs as well. But when it's a script for autocue you can see he's a good writer; he's a good journalist.

'So there I am saying, "Oh jeez, I wish I could do that" and I didn't realize that Des was there and he heard me say it. He came over and said, "Look, it's all very well me having all that nicely written and everything, but the guy at home will listen to you because you have the authority of actually having been out there at the pinnacle of sport. You stick to what you do well. You played in three hundred-odd games for Arsenal, you played in Cup Finals.

' "If you turn round and say it's going to be really diffi-cult today," or, "You've got to wear these sort of studs because of so-and-so," people at home will immediately say, "Yeah, that's right, never thought of that." '

'He was basically saying: stick to what I know best which is credibility on the football front, sporting back-ground, and knowing how athletes, sportsmen, feel on the big occasion. I realized I would definitely be able to feel credible about any sport. I know what it feels like to be in competition, what the competitive element feels like as a sportsman.

'It was a really important thing he did for me at that time. In other words, he was saying don't try to be like Des Lynam, don't try to be like Hugh McIlvanny with beautiful words just waiting to come out; just be yourself. My area of expertise was being a former professional and that was just as valid as anyone else's area of expertise.'

Wilson's move to ITV after World Cup USA in 1994 paid off and BBC sports staff – Des included – were left angry and frustrated at losing some major sporting highlights to their rivals both at ITV and on satellite television. Des used to say that there was nothing he liked better than being up against ITV and giving them a good kicking in the ratings. Suddenly that all changed.
Wilson says:

'ITV were looking to broaden their expertise after USA 94 and they were looking for more credibility. I think they had had quite a bad World Cup in some ways and suddenly I was presented with an opportunity.

'As it happens, [the move] has turned out better than good for me. I had what I wanted: *the* seat. And we've got the big games.

'The Champions League is a big project for the next four years, and next season we will be producing seventeen Wednesday matches live and covering thirty games in all.

'The fact that the FA Cup came to ITV as well vindicated my decision to move. Des was very upset. I think losing the FA Cup upset them more than anything else.'

Wilson also has some other harsh words for his former BBC employers.

'Studio presentation now is fairly boring but I love being at the event and that's where, particularly at the moment, we are showing people that we can cut the mustard. We like to be at the event. In a studio you have all the controls and autocue and all that, but at the World Cup in 1998 in France we were out on the road, hanging on the edge of a stand or a balcony, and with all the noise and speaker systems and everything else adding to the atmosphere.

'Some people like to see this sort of situation and some of them said, 'Oh, at least you were at the events.' I do believe that ITV were *at* the World Cup and the BBC were *nearly* at the World Cup.

'They had the controlled studio situation and they did not get any of the atmosphere. You don't get atmosphere sitting in a comfortable five-star hotel in Paris. I was actually very critical of the BBC about that, but that's not to say the people sitting at home didn't enjoy it. With Des fronting it, and Alan Hansen's analysis so good, they had a very strong hand in that way.

'But, I think what we did was brave and some people said they thought it was fantastic.'

Wilson says he gets at least four letters a week from people asking: How can I become the next Des Lynam? He tells them that Des began in local newspapers and local radio, moved onto national BBC radio and gained a terrific background through what is now Radio 5, and ensured a natural progression.

'There are very few people that I know who have a bad word to say about him on the broadcast side. He has had a hard route up. In the same way I had to struggle as an amateur footballer and then fought my way from being in Arsenal reserves, Des had all that side to him, too. Through local radio, local newspapers, national radio he won his spurs. Earned his place.

'Television is a hugely competitive business. I used to say that about footbal, but the great thing about football is that if I played well in goal I would have to be picked next week. And once I made a reputation as an international, unless I had a run of five or six nightmare games, there was no way I was going to be replaced.

'But if you are in the television business, if someone doesn't like your face, you are out. Only a handful of TV presenters can honestly sleep soundly in their beds at night knowing they would not be replaced, and one of them is Des Lynam. He can sleep happily.

'When I used to get quite agitated about the situation I was in as the permanent substitute, my daughter Anna, who was fighting against cancer, said, "Dad, it doesn't matter." But it does to me.

'I think Des understands that. When Anna died, one of the first letters came from Des. We meet from time to time and we'll joke. During Euro 96, the BBC made a great play of having the semi-final between England and Germany and an audience of 19.6 or 20 million or whatever. But in the World Cup two years later it was our turn. We had England versus Argentina and with 26.5 million viewers, the biggest audience ever on an individual channel in the history of television. We laughed, but it was our turn to have the stroke of luck.'

Wilson is inevitably compared with Des – perhaps more so since he left the BBC than when he was the unwilling Number Two.

But he is happy with the knowledge that what he offers is different from Des and he's not short of a compliment or two for his rival. 'I feel quite comfortable now throwing in my two-penn'orth off the cuff,' says Wilson,

'but Des is different. Part of his skill is in the way he reacts to people. Autocue gets you into and out of programmes but the ability to listen to argument and react to it, as well as taking in all the other instructions through your earpiece, that's what makes Des special.

'It's the ease with which he does it. People feel comfortable. You don't ever really think he's going to look embarrassing. In Italy in 1990 – the famous time when he dried up – I was in the studio. Des got the screen and he suddenly lost the plot, which we have all done, I can tell you.

'You can't explain it. Something just happens. It might be a tannoy going off somewhere, or a fire alarm sounding in the studio. Once I was in the studio with Jimmy Hill when a fire alarm did go off and he shouted out, "What's that?" Des would probably have laughed at it and said, "Oh, that's my mother phoning in," or something, you know.

'But anyway, in Italy, Des suddenly lost the plot and we all looked at one another and thought, "This isn't right. It's Des."

'He was mortified, but it helped all of us, I can tell you that. It showed he was human. It helped me, because I thought, "If that can happen to Des Lynam . . ." '

The incident has never been forgotten by the hyper self-critical Des. It sticks in his mind despite the many instances where we could all point to Des saving the day when circumstances out of a broadcaster's control have taken effect – like in the Grand National that never was or the race cancelled because of a bomb threat.

But, no, Des recalls the nightmare of being stuck in front of a live camera, mouth gaping but without the usual flow of polished words cascading forth: 'You coast along thinking you've got this business cracked then . . . disaster. Don't know why that happened. I'd had to do a live trail a few minutes before, when I'd had to remember a lot of things. And they'd moved the broadcast position just before I went on because the Italians had been complaining about where we were standing. So I was pretty harassed. But I lost my concentration. Just went. In front of fourteen million people.'

He always refers to the incident as: 'See Naples and dry.' Another fine example of the Lynam wit. Des is famed for rarely making mistakes, but there have been one or two other howlers. In an early boxing broadcast, he earnestly told radio listeners: '. . . born in Italy, all his fights have been in his native New York.' And once, on *Grandstand*, as the teleprinter clattered away, he announced the result: Chesterfield 1, Chester 1,' before adding, 'another score draw there in that local derby . . .'

Wilson adds:

'That's the other great thing, his humour. Des can be so funny. I remember Kenny Dalglish and me being on a particular game as the experts. Des came on and said, "Our experts tonight are two guys who between them have won 106 caps for Scotland. Kenny Dalglish who has won 104 and Bob Wilson who has won two."

'He just put me away. I had only played my second cap when I got the injury that finished my career so I only ever got those two caps. Somebody had put Des up to it, I'm sure, but things like that he delivers so brilliantly. You just have to laugh and get on with it. There's no way back from a comment like that. Afterwards I didn't stop laughing for I don't know how long.

'The one word you have got to put against Des Lynam, though, is style. For anybody to copy Des would be a disaster area. The TV eye is all-seeing. If you are anxious it will show. If you are feeling bad it will show. Des has the style not to let anything show.

'There's also a certain element of women who adore him. He's got the style, a great voice, lots of charm. I have never seen him being rude, or angry and he has never been moody. If I could level anything at him – and it's frustrating for someone like me who has had to work for everything whether it be in football or on TV – it is that if anything, it comes so easy to him. He is such a natural that he can be a little bit lazy at times.

'Where I would be double and treble checking this, that and the other, Des would not be doing that because he did not think it would be necessary.

'He also has an economy with words. If I have learnt anything particularly from Des it is an economy of words. That's something he has made me realize – the impact of a few well-chosen words. That and to try to get a nice little line that finishes off a programme and leaves people with something to think about.'

And, crucially, to deliver that nice little line without a hiccup. Des's unruffled delivery has also been an inspiration to Wilson who once, he quite happily recalls, came out with the wonderfully mangled phrase: 'He's pissed a fatness test'.

Colleague, boss of, and more importantly friend of Des for many years is Brian Barwick, head of sport at ITV and, until the end of 1998 head of sport at the BBC. He laughs:

'Desmond and I have shared a curry in every major city in the world.

'I have done all the big events with Des. I have done Olympics with him and World Cups with him and *Sports Review of the Year* with him and, I suppose, of the shows I did he had to be the presenter for the last eight or nine years I was at the BBC, so we spent hours and hours and hours together.

'I found him a fantastic guy to work with. He is a good bloke. He's the sort of fella you can have a bit of fun with. He's a very sharp professional so you can enjoy the professional moments as well. I certainly enjoyed some fantastic professional moments with him because I felt confident in my bit and I knew he was competent in his bit, so you tended to be able to push back the boundaries. You were both confident that if you got yourself into trouble on the air you could get yourself out of trouble.

131

'We did some broadcasts where you came off fairly warm about them. And, of course, you could have a decent night out at the end of them with Desmond. I have a great warm regard for him.'

When Brian was made editor of *Match of the Day*, almost his first thought was to lure Des Lynam away from *Grandstand* to present the programme. He says:

'I started working with Des in the early 1980s. When I became the editor of *Match of the Day* I persuaded him to come and join our team. He has a great love of football – that and the appeal of the show probably suited him at the time.

'He had worked on *Grandstand* for some considerable time and had done all the big days and I think he fancied changing horses. It was a new era for *Match of the Day* and Des fit the bill perfectly.

'He still did the Olympics, he still did Wimbledon, he still did the Grand National, so he still was able to work on the Blue Riband events whilst changing his core activity.'

One of their early shows together encompassed the terrible tragedy of Hillsborough. It was a difficult programme for everyone involved, but it was a programme where Des's excellent journalistic credentials were amply illustrated. Brian says:

'Des and Jimmy Hill, who were due to appear on the programme, had actually gone up to see the game. They were going to come back and present the programme in London having seen the game. So, in the end, they also saw the difficulties first hand.

'In terms of the programme you got a strong journalistic brief from Desmond which was also allied to the fact that he had been there. You got a first-hand account.

'Anybody who underrates Desmond as a journalist is underrating him in a considerable fashion. One of the things that used to make his blood boil, and used to make my blood boil, was when people used to say occasionally of our output together that there wasn't enough journalism in it. In truth, you are interpreting live events on the air and you are actually being journalistic about something that people have a real feel for and understanding of, and if you interpret it the wrong way people will soon tell you.

'It's quite a clinical and difficult art, live sports broad-casting, and you are interpreting the facts as they are appearing before your very eyes. A good example of that would be the two major Grand National situations – the false start and the IRA bomb threat – where Desmond had to interpret on the air as these events unfolded. So, he's a very strong journalist and I think also he's a great prepara-tion man.

'What people see is just the tip of the iceberg when they see him perform. There's years of experience and there's hours of thinking going into each broadcast. And then, with all that bedrock of knowledge and understanding about what is about to be broadcast, he can actually free himself up to do the broadcast itself comfortably because he can always fall back on the knowledge if he has to.

'He is the best there has ever been, in my opinion. He's in a league of one in terms of sports broadcasters – not just because of his experience and good grounding in radio. He was a developing talent in television when I first knew him. He didn't start the way he has finished. He learned along the way.

'He got very confident because he has done plenty of hours. A lot of sports broadcasting is about how many hours you have got under the bonnet really. And there's also a natural charm, professionalism and style which was given freedom to develop and he has become very comfortable with the medium.'

One of Brian's favourite memories of Des was their collabora-tion before the World Cup in Italy in 1990 which eventually had a bigger impact on the nation than either of them could have realized at the time. At a time when most people would have thought 'Nessun Dorma' was a campervan made by a Japanese car company, Brian and Des somehow managed to pick this opera classic as the theme tune for their World Cup coverage.

Brian says:

'We would claim jointly to have changed social culture in the UK by picking "Nessun Dorma" as the theme tune for the World Cup in 1990.

'We were looking for a theme song for the World Cup in 1990 and because it was in Italy we were getting all manner of things sent into us and a lot of them sounded like *It's A Knockout* themes really. We both recognised that it needed some style and status.

'Then Des came up with Pavarotti who, to my eternal shame, I had only just about heard of, and he said he thought that Pavarotti singing "O Sole Mio" might be good. But to me, that was the wrong song because it was also the theme for an advertising slogan, "Just One Cornetto", at the time. I thought it was the wrong song but the right singer. It was a bloody good call with "O Sole Mio" but because of the Cornetto thing we needed another song and I came up with "Nessun Dorma".

'In many ways we got ourselves into something that became a monster and changed, in a very modest way, people's perception of classical music and opera. People were whistling it who had never heard of it before.'

The tune certainly caught on. Even now most people could call it to mind if given a nudge. And the record company which released the tune was extremely grateful to Des and Brian for plucking it from relative obscurity.

'Four years later we were in Los Angeles at the Three Tenors concert which ended the World Cup in America,' says Brian.

'We managed to get tickets for this concert and we had a night of magic under the stars in the LA Dodgers' stadium. We went in together and went beyond row, beyond row, beyond row to find our seats. And we went beyond people like Tom Cruise, Arnold Shwarzenegger, Whoopi Goldberg, Louis Jordan, Walter Matthau, a couple of retired Presidents and eventually we sat down.

'We weren't far away from a group of people who were walking in straight past what looked like three eminent old gentlemen so we joined the throng of people and we walked past too, and it was Bob Hope, Frank Sinatra and Gene Kelly – not a bad inside forward line!

'I think we got the tickets through the record company so we have always had a very warm glow about "Nessun Dorma".'

But, like Bob Wilson, Brian eventually left the BBC for ITV. And he can understand Des's frustrations with the corporation.

He says:

'Scheduling of *Match of the Day* was always a problem. We always felt it was on too late. I think, to be fair, that the schedulers knew that and the Controller of BBC knew that, but its placing was almost a product of what had gone before. To put the jigsaw in the right place for programmes earlier in the evening then sometimes programmes at the back end were shunted later.

'There was also the problem from the schedulers' perception that this programme did very well at a certain time of night so there was an argument to say it's doing very well at this time of night, it might not do so well at a different time of night.

'That was a difficult one to sell when you started a programme called *Match of the Day* and ended it by saying that was the match of yesterday because it had gone beyond midnight.

'In the end I left because I got a great offer to come to ITV but equally I felt that, perhaps, the great days of BBC sport were behind them rather than ahead of them, simply because the market had changed significantly; and that I doubted their ability to stay in the game at the very highest level in some of the sports that I was most keen to be involved in.

'I suppose, in a way, recognition of that is as recent as the FA Cup Final in May 1999 which was live on ITV and Sky, and the Champions League Final which was live on ITV. They were two occasions that in the past would have found time on the BBC.'

A peak audience of 18.8 million watched the dramatic Champions League Final between Manchester United and Bayern Munich live from Barcelona. Manchester United, who last won the old European Cup in 1968, had the whole country behind them as they challenged for the title again. And they won in the most extraordinary circumstances, with first an equalizer and then a winning goal both in stoppage time at the end of the game. It was one of the most dramatic sporting moments seen on television for many years.

'I left because I just felt it was time,' Brian Barwick concludes ruefully. 'There was a potential of my being a King Canute figure. There was an inevitablity about it. I hope that changes because a strong BBC sports department is good for the industry.'

8

Dry and *Great Smelling*

'My whole approach is based on the idea that, in the end,
it is only sport.'

– Des Lynam

Suave and debonair are words which conjure up images of the
1970s when Tony Curtis and Roger Moore were *The Persuaders*,
and curly perms made thousands of men, especially footballers,
look like French poodles. Strange, then, that these two words
are still often used to describe Des Lynam – when we're not
referring to him as 'dishy Des' that is.

In terms of style, though, you couldn't say that he's stuck in
a timewarp. Maybe the moustache – a bit Jason King even now
– is dated but, otherwise, you've got to say that Des is the epit-
ome of what should, in tribute to him, be called the Sports
Presenter Look. His clothes are stylish without being flash,
smart without being trendy, unless Harris tweed is this season's
latest look, and the overall picture says: Money, style, taste. He's
understated and leisurely, relaxed yet confidently powerful.

The combination helps to give him his legendary sex appeal,
according to Jane Lawless from the Motcombs Club. She says:
'His sex appeal comes from being very cuddly, very masculine
and combining that butch moustache with the tweed jacket. He
has a very sexy voice and he makes you feel the epicentre of
everything. He gives you his undivided attention.'

A creature of habits, Des tends to buy most of his sports jackets and slacks from an emporium in Marylebone, London,

which could have provided the inspiration for comedian Paul Whitehouse's hilarious creation, the over-the-top tailor. 'Ooh, suits *you*, sir.' He takes along his partner Rose, sometimes, for guidance but generally he's a man who knows what he wants. 'I buy five or six jackets a year,' he says, 'but I'm only interested in clothes from a professional point of view.'

That's true. Mr Suits You Sir reveals that: 'Mr Lynam comes in at least twice a season and he always reminds us that his jackets should not pick up on camera when he's on television. I mean, you see some people on TV whose jackets make you think your horizontal hold has gone. He's always the first person we invite to see our new season's clothes and to get his sizes and everything.'

It's a fact that all television presenters, these days, have to be extra careful about their wardrobe. The modern way in which a background is often projected on to a screen, rather like a 'virtual set', means that those who work in front of the camera must avoid certain colours. When *Match of the Day* first adopted this technique, Des wasn't allowed to wear anything with green in. 'Had to be careful,' he says. 'Because of the backdrop we can't wear green ourselves. That wouldn't be seen. Instead you would see the transmitted picture. I've got an awful lot of ties that have a speck of green, or a line or a stripe. I have two wardrobes, a match day and a non-match day collection.'

The moustache has been part of Des's facial furniture since 1973 when he decided to grow a beard while on holiday, and it's now unlikely ever to be removed. 'I had the full beard for about four months,' says Des, 'but you never feel really clean, do you? So, I took it off but I left the moustache. The *Viva Zapata* look was quite fashionable then. I've tried shaving it off a couple of times on holidays since but I just don't feel myself when I shave it off, so I hurriedly grow it back. I haven't got anything dodgy on my upper lip or anything, it's just that I feel happier with the moustache.'

In his many ventures away from the sporting arena some have been extremely successful, some less so. But Des's taste and style have always made him a perfect vehicle for advertisers. He has refused to exploit this as ferociously as many in his position might. But there have been a few examples where his fans are suddenly jolted by the sight of Des's smiling face peering from some unlikely hoarding or newspaper advert.

Or even the classic television campaign he filmed for Right Guard deodorant. Des, the man who's so dry he parted the Red Sea like Moses. That clever campaign caught the mood of the moment – that football was the new religion and Des was its God. It was all ironic, of course, but Des was more than happy to send himself up. 'What, you want me to be dry *and* great smelling?' he says quizzically to the unseen director. It's a vital element of the ad. What is really happening is that here's Des Lynam slumming it a bit to get some extra dosh, but because he doesn't take himself seriously we can accept it as Des Lynam the sports commentator doing a bit of moonlighting. For a fee rumoured to be around £80,000, of course.

Accepting the element of self-parody is inevitable if you are going to get into that kind of advertising. You cannot appear to be taking yourself too seriously when you are obviously selling yourself. Not that self parody would ever be a problem for Des. His advanced sense of humour has been a feature throughout his career but even his good friend, impressionist Rory Bremner, who takes him off superbly from time to time, was surprised at how willing Des was to appear on his show and actually take the rise out of himself.

When Bremner recruited Des to film a link for his show he found, to his surprise, that Des was quite a talent. 'He just had to do it straight,' says Bremner, 'but he suddenly started to overload it with Des-isms. He was doing it just to take the piss out of himself, and I've always admired him for that. He was also particularly good at it.'

Arthur Smith was also surprised at how happy Des was to ham it up for the sake of comedic impact in *My Summer with Des*. Des loved being part of it all but later confided: 'I was playing Des rather than being Des – although, of course, there's not a vast difference between the two.'

One advertising creative director says:

'Des Lynam is great for the right products. Celebrities are chosen not because an individual at Gillette or wherever likes them but because they research well. Des is such a likeable chap but more importantly research would have shown that women like him, that certain targeted sections of the community like him; that his recognition factor will highlight a product. When you are spending a lot of money on a big campaign with a celebrity like Desmond Lynam, research is crucial.

'The fact that he only appears to have started making money from advertisements in more recent years is no great surprise. He would have faced restrictions from within the BBC in years gone by, when he would not have been allowed to do certain types of ads. Now things have changed, and there's greater flexibility.

'I am sure many companies would have loved to use Des Lynam but the BBC have always been very strict with their artists, that anything they do should in no way conflict with their main BBC role. It would have been a case of finding out could he do something; would he like to do it and then, crucially, that he would have scored highly in research.'

One company delighted to find that Des scores in research even better than his television protégé Gary Lineker used to score on the football field were the makers of Miracle Gro fertilizer. Des was so successful in trials that he was snapped up for an amazing eleven-year deal to front the product. All Des has to do is hold a box of the fabled concoction and, hey presto, sales graphs go into rocket mode. And when he advertised Boddingtons beer during one of the World Cups, more than 100 life-size cardboard cutouts of him were stolen from pubs and bars around the country.

They can't all have ended up in one of the students' bars at Warwick University which was once famously renamed the Des Lynam Lounge.

There have been voiceovers for Lucozade and car companies and a lucrative in-flight advertising film for British Airways, but probably Des's first excursion into the world of advertising came when he posed for the glossy pages – not of *Hello!* magazine – but of the Freemans Catalogue. The ideal home, you might think, for the pin-up of the nation's sporting couch potatoes. How sensible. You can order, from the comfort of your favourite armchair, a nice track suit to watch *Match of the Day* in. Freemans offered him an attractive five-year deal to promote their leisure wear at the start of the 1990s.

One of London's top photographers, Jeany Savage, was recruited to take the snaps which would turn Des into a fashion model. And she was soon impressed by his overwhelming charm. The team flew to Portugal twice a year to shoot the picture sets and Jeany, a down-to-earth, no-nonsense East End girl recalls with a laugh: 'Des and I met doing the Freemans Catalogue shoots. He's a nice bloke, lovely sense of humour and all that, but he's tight as arseholes. He was getting £45,000 a year for a couple of photo shoots but he never had to put his hand in his pocket. Every time we went to a bar it was "Oh Mr Lynam . . . on the house". He loved that. He never paid for anything. He never bought a drink the whole time we were there.'

The photo shoot team had a terrific time – mainly thanks to Des's easy-going manner and cracking sense of humour, says Jeany. 'We used to laugh all the time. He's wicked. As a model he would do this pose, a sort of comic . . . "On my life . . . Oh, my boy . . ." you know. And then he would do all his impersonations.

'His Michael Caine was perfect and he did a terrific Frank Spencer as well. He is very entertaining. Very, very good company.'

During the shoots, mainly for knitwear and sportswear, which took place in January/February and again in July, Des and Jeany and the stylists would go for meals together and after a couple of gin and tonics and a glass or two of red wine, Des would turn on the old charm.

'He is a ladykiller who flirts with everybody,' laughs Jeany.

'He used to always chat me up, silly old sod. I remember one night he asked me to go back to his room but we were laughing so much I didn't take him seriously. I just used to lead him on. I would say to him, "Who are you flirting with, you silly old fool."

'One night in Portugal I popped round to his room to see him about something or other and he was lying on the bed snoring away like a trooper. I just thought, "If all those people who dream about you could see you like that . . ."

'I got the impression that he fell for me big time. I went out with him a couple of times when we came back home but we were never together in that sense, you know. Whatever happened he would always return to Rose.'

As for Des's fashion sense, Jeany recalls: 'He wears good clothes but they are so boring, really. He loves ties and I used to buy nice ones for him. After the Freemans shoots I would say, "Do you want these?" because he could have taken the samples home if he liked, and he would look at them and say, "No thanks, maybe you can take them home for your dad." The money he got for those shoots used to pay for his holidays.'

During the 1980s Des brought his charm, personality and public profile to the world of public relations. He became a director of CPR, a public relations firm set up and run by his friend Peter Creasey. They had offices in Fleet Street, London, before moving out to plush new premises on the Isle of Dogs in London's docklands.

The company helped to promote the image of quite a mixed portfolio of companies including the sports shoemakers Hi Tech and various firms from the worlds of property and construction. It started out as a straight PR firm, but moved into the arena of sports sponsorship with help from Des.

One former account executive recalls:

'I had lunch a few times with Des and Peter Creasey. In fact, I remember having lunch at Des's house when things were starting to look a little gloomy for the company as we discussed ways to improve matters.

'Des was made a director of CPR but he didn't get involved at all in the day-to-day affairs of the company. It was good for the company, though, to have someone of

Des's stature on board and we would wheel him out now and again to help close a deal or for a big publicity launch. He was very impressive at publicity launches, as you might expect, and he would compere the event or what-ever.

'We only saw him, perhaps, half a dozen times a year but he was always a pleasure to deal with. I think part of his deal was that we gave him a new BMW every couple of years.'

With Des's added credibility factor, the company persuaded Hi Tech to sponsor the British Open squash championships for a while, and followed that by persuading Davies and Tate, an Eastbourne-based double glazing outfit to take over the spon-sorship.

However, the company was one of the early casualties of the recession in the late 1980s and finally was forced to close. The former executive says: 'It was a shame. During the recession everyone cut back on their marketing budgets and we lost some clients. Then a couple of members of staff left and took their clients with them and before you knew it we were out of busi-ness.'

Another former member of staff recalls: 'It was a nice little company to work for and whenever Des came into the office he was always very cheerful and charming. He came to our Christmas party and he has that knack of making everyone he talks to feel just a little bit special. We had this thing that every-one had to buy someone else in the company a Christmas present costing not more than £5. I remember that Des's girl-friend bought me a set of make-up brushes which was rather sweet.'

Des is no stranger to winning awards, although he was a little surprised when his affection for neckwear, spotted by photo-grapher Jeany Savage, led to him receiving the ultimate broad-casters' accolade in 1992. He was nominated as one of the Top 20 tie wearers in Britain by the British Guild of Tiemakers!

Over the years, he has garnered an impressive collection of more serious awards. He was voted TV Sports Presenter of the

Year in 1985, '86, '88, '92 and '97 and topped the poll of a *Radio Times* search for the Male TV Personality of the Year in 1989. He was given the Richard Dimbleby Award from the British Academy of Film and Television Arts (BAFTA) in 1995 for the year's most important contribution on screen in factual television. It is a highly prized honour which is in the gift of the BAFTA council.

That Des is happiest and at his best in his world of sport is obvious, but it is only natural that the BBC should have wanted to try to make full use of one of their greatest assets and try him out in different areas. However, not everything he touches turns into a ratings success.

There have also been several attempts to turn Des into a chat show host – none of which has been entirely successful. Towards the end of the 1980s he was lined up for an afternoon show on BBC 1, an attempt to make him a sort of daytime Terry Wogan, which Des described as more of a *Desert Island Discs* for television. Over the years he has made other pilots along these lines but they always seemed to be lacking in one respect or another.

He has turned down other prime avenues for his talents; rejecting an offer to front *Crimewatch UK* ahead of Nick Ross – predicting that it would be a one-season wonder – and steering away from offers for breakfast television, including an approach from GMTV. On radio he took part in the comedy show *They Think It's All Over* with Rory McGrath and Rory Bremner, but turned down the chance to follow the show onto television, saying modestly that he didn't think he was funny enough.

One area where he did enjoy some success, but ultimately wasn't happy in the environment, was in travel. He very nearly didn't have to worry about paying for holidays for quite some time when he agreed to host the BBC's *Holiday* programme. He first flirted with travel show presenting in 1982 when he was lined up to present several episodes of BBC 2's *The Travel Show* with Isla St Clair, the girl who found fame on the *Generation Game*. But it was as presenter of *Holiday '89* that viewers mostly remember him.

Des was handed the holiday hotseat when revelations about

the private life of former host Frank Bough, whom Des had followed into television sport, forced Bough to leave the show. It was a very real chance to spread his wings and move into a new, glamorous arena, but one which he chose not to pursue. There was some pressure put on Des to capitalize on his 'Dishy Des' image to do swimwear shots to boost the show's ratings and he later confessed to having mixed feelings about the show's 'soft, polite tone'.

Rejecting an offer to host more series, Des reflected: 'I like a bit of travelling but I hate tourism. Tourists spoil places, they don't ever add to them.' Not exactly the required sentiments of a holiday show presenter. Des also spotted another unwanted side-effect of a potential switch to more general television presenting. 'I had been in sports broadcasting for twenty-three years but people immediately thought of me as the holiday man,' he mused.

In recent years, his most memorable diversion was to host the BBC's look-behind-the-scenes factual programme, *How Do They Do That?* The essence of the programme was to entertain viewers by unravelling the mind-boggling detail and background behind some of the world's most unusual events and human achievements – while also lifting the lid on some of the special effects which bamboozle film and television audiences into believing the evidence of their own eyes.

One of television's natural cynics himself, Des was delighted to be part of *How Do They Do That?*, which he co-hosted with Jenny Hull, because it was uplifting and positive. He says: 'The great thing about *How Do They Do That?* was that it was so positive I actually found it heartening – especially the stories we tackled about people pulling through against the odds. It's nice to be able to tell people exactly how they did that. The show was not trashy, not a game of any sort, yet it had a smile in there, too.'

Some of the questions answered by the series came from viewers, but at least one was born out of Des's own curiosity. He says: 'I've always wanted to know exactly how air traffic controllers work, so we featured them in the show. It was absolutely fascinating – mind you I'm not saying it has made me more relaxed and reassured when I fly. Having seen what they have to do, I'm probably more nervous than ever.'

The series started in the autumn of 1993 and finally ran for a total of sixty-six episodes over the next four years. It was divided into five sub series, plus compilations. Des presented the first two sub series, totalling thirty shows. His co-host, newcomer Jenny Hull, was a pretty and articulate foil to Des's laconic humour. Together they introduced each item and voiced the commentaries for each video segment. They also took part in some of the stunts and certain live studio items.

One of the show's production team says: 'The shows were originally conceived in the US as "feel-good" entertainment with a solid factual base in technical achievement, but always with an emphasis on the individual human stories behind the achievement. It was a completely new style of show for British TV, with a huge studio set in BBC's Studio One and a live audience. There were seven items in each three-quarter-of-an-hour show; six on tape and one live in the studio.'

The range of *How do they?* topics covered was enormous. They included how special effects were achieved in then current films, like *The Fugitive* or *Free Willie,* or in advertisements, like the free-ranging Esso Tigers or the house built of living people in the Halifax Building Society ads, or the then famous 'dancing milk bottles'.

There were also many items featuring animals, such as one on how sniffer dogs were selected and trained, or successful efforts to save rare breeds like the Californian Condor. There were revolutionary medical treatments which included the use of traffic spotting computer systems to identify fertile human sperm for couples having difficulty conceiving, or total lung transplants.

Then there were the technical stories; how the TV ratings are gathered; how the new rollercoaster in Blackpool was built and designed; how an aircraft carrier functions; how they built the Channel Tunnel; how the live power lines across Britain are maintained; how the aircraft 'black box' works, etc, etc.

The production team member recalls:

'These latter technical stories were Des's favourites, although one of the most successful items was a live studio interview with his old friend Rory Bremner who showed him how to do various impressions. It turned out that Des was actually very good at it. Rory even did one of Des himself which was hilarious!

'The first series did phenomenally well, pushing into the Top 10 with figures around 10 million. Later series settled down a bit to the sevens and eight millions, but the show was certainly enormously well known. "How do they do that then?" became a national catch phrase for a while.'

As part of the introduction for the first series, Des himself had to film a hair-raising stunt from a helicopter, high above the BBC Television Centre at White City, in London. Des was seen peering from the helicopter, the wind blowing through his immaculate moustache and hair before he leapt out of the chopper without a parachute and crash landed spectacularly through the studio roof.

It was, of course, a clever sky-diving stunt and the programme revealed exactly how Des did that. But he admits that filming his own part in the stunning sequence really did put the wind up him. He says: 'I really did leap out of the helicopter but the way it was put together was a carefully crafted optical illusion. I am not madly keen on heights and I hate helicopters – especially ones which have no door on my side. I was told that my insurance had been bumped up for the occasion so my dependants would have been OK if anything had gone wrong. Frankly, I was more worried about me at the time.'

The show insider adds:

'The whole point of these stunts was to ask How Did They Do That? afterwards and show just how well planned and safe they were.

'The second stunt was much more ambitious. Jenny appeared to drive a car with Des as the horrified passenger in a wild stunt-packed car chase which involved another vehicle turning over and their car losing its roof under an articulated lorry – the car finally falling to pieces at the studio. It was great fun for all of us and Des enjoyed it all enormously.'

During filming of the second series, however, Des became restless and in the end, he decided to leave. *GMTV*'s smooth breakfast presenter Eamonn Holmes was drafted in to take the show on to two further successful series.

Why did Des decide to leave such a popular show? It was a mystery to the production team who felt that he was certainly happy with the show. The feeling behind the scenes was that the whole production team got on unusually well and there was always a great atmosphere whether the cameras were rolling or not.

The reasoning behind his departure was probably quite complex in that he was, perhaps, faced with a difficult decision. *How Do They Do That?* had exposed him to a whole new audience and broadened his identity – more than even he realized – yet he was still fully committed to his first love, sport. That meant he had a considerable work load and faced the choice between going forward to a new broader identity – and a lot more work hours – or returning to what he really loved best.

It was not the first time Des had tried something new; enjoyed the experience and the success, but then decided that if it meant compromising his love of sport he would rather walk away. He has himself said that if he had been younger he might have seized new opportunities more vigorously. But in the case of *How Do They Do That?*, why should he?

Des, of course, has made himself the master of sports presenting. But what is the job of the television link-man? What makes Des so good at it?

An executive on *How Do They Do That?* reckons:

'For a link-man like Des, it's a bit like juggling. They have to think of several things at once. Live presenters do develop the most extraordinary skill at listening to the producer while also listening to the interviewee, but I think over the years Des has developed considerable editorial skills of his own and probably doesn't need much prompting from a producer.

'Certainly on *How Do They Do That?* we didn't use an earpiece with him at all. The other great skill they develop of course is timing – sensing the natural rhythm of an interview. He's able to work very precisely. If you say to Des, "Give 'em a wind-up lasting twelve seconds from now," you will get a smooth relaxed and apparently spontaneous piece lasting exactly . . . twelve seconds.'

On shows which are entirely scripted there is less pressure on the presenter but, even then, we can all think of some television 'face' or other who appears to have trouble reading the autocue let alone handling sudden changes, breakdowns or the need to ad-lib. For programmes like *Points of View*, which Des sometimes presents, he will write his own script, as he always does, and if the autocue broke down he wouldn't miss a beat.

In the 'live' television environment, it would be easy to find your working life crushingly demanding. It calls for accuracy and attention to detail combined with an acute sense of timing. When your working role is so pressurized and demanding of professional standards it is easy to gain a reputation as a control freak. Des certainly enjoys this reputation amongst certain colleagues at the BBC. One colleague told me: 'Des can be quite difficult at times. It's not that he's awkward or being a prima donna or anything like that, but he does hold strong opinions on how certain things should be done and, let's say, he likes to have his way.'

Before I began researching material for this book, I sought permission to go behind the scenes on *Match of the Day* to write a feature which was destined to appear in a national daily newspaper. At the time there wasn't a problem. But once I began to work on the biography, my access to *Match of the Day* was suddenly refused for the reason, I can only assume, that Des's BBC executive chums were worried I might ask them to comment on Des. When I asked why I couldn't visit the *Match of the Day* studios, a kindly BBC insider told me: 'If Des says

"No" the BBC portcullis comes down, it's as simple as that.' I wouldn't mind, but the programme I was scheduled to watch in the making had Gary Lineker in the hot seat, not Des. Still, I was given a prime example of Des's power behind the scenes.

In all my research, I experienced three types of response from those I approached to contribute towards this book. The majority were delighted to assist and to add their voice and recollections to the phenomenon which is Des Lynam. One or two weren't sure because Des was 'a mate'. And one or two others said they would have liked to help but they were clearly worried about stepping on Des's toes.

Veteran commentator John Motson told me: 'I wish you well but I'm sorry I can't help you personally. Des has asked that I don't get involved.' Alan Hansen said pretty much the same and dear old Jimmy Hill said, 'I would have liked to have helped but Des has asked me not to and I've got to stick by my mate.' Happily many others were delighted to help compile this biography which is, in many ways, a tribute to Des.

Even though the occasional knock-back made my task more difficult, I probably wouldn't call Des's tendency – his need, perhaps – to control a particular character fault as such. It is one of the character traits which has taken him to the top. He knows that he needs to be in control. An effective presenter needs to come across that way. It is why we can put our trust in Des to deliver and to cope no matter what. Both viewers and his employers have faith in him. They can see his confidence and competence. Others can interpret this as 'he's a control freak'.

There is, of course, another side to the coin. A generosity of spirit and willingness to be of help to those less gifted or, perhaps, just newer to the demands of television. One senior BBC figure, editor of a flagship programme, told me how Des was extremely supportive when he was seconded to BBC Sport as a relative new boy to the corporation. He says:

'I'll never forget the first day. I walked in – and you know how nerve-wracking it can be on the first day in any job – and there was Des, this legendary figure of sports broadcasting, and various other sports department guys. Des was the first to welcome me on board and he really took the trouble to make me feel comfortable. I think he understands how we can all be a little nervous and, as a youngster, he wanted to put me at my ease. In all the time I worked with him I can honestly say I never heard anyone have a bad word for him and I personally think he's a superb bloke. A genuinely nice guy.'

He can be touchy, though. Just how touchy he can be about his image was amply illustrated by two profiles which appeared in no less than the erudite *Times* and *Sunday Times* in May and July of World Cup year, 1998. *The Times* article quoted an amusing, yet harmless, anecdote from Matthew Lorenzo, a sports presenter with Sky television. In it, Lorenzo revealed how he met Des at a party to celebrate the BBC's opening night coverage of a previous World Cup. Lorenzo was anchor man for ITV's coverage at the time and Lorenzo recalled how Des took him to one side and said: 'Matthew, let me tell you what is going to happen. They will put you up against me, and I'll win. That's the way it is. Keep your head down and enjoy yourself.'

Lorenzo told this story as an example of Des's generosity of spirit, adding that Des had been the soul of modesty in saying what he had. The gist of it was that Des was saying 'Don't worry about the viewing figures, mate. Just enjoy the tournament'.

However, when the *Sunday Times* repeated the anecdote in a separate profile, it appeared that Des was being somewhat less than modest. Boastful, even. It was enough to send him screaming into action and a call was quickly made to News International, owners of the newspapers, from Des's legal representative.

A News International executive revealed:

'He's Teflon man, isn't he, but he's still incredibly jealous of his reputation. He had that whole thing about his relationship all over the newspapers during the World Cup, but he got away with it scot free. And he felt the need to take action over something fairly innocuous like this.

'*The Times* article was fine but the *Sunday Times* profile put a different spin on the same incident. He contacted us through lawyers and we agreed we would not use the quote again as it appeared in the *Sunday Times*. We agreed to amend the files. It was such a minor frisson of criticism in an article that was otherwise so flattering. He would have looked foolish if we'd been forced to publish an apology. It was an irritating little complaint but one he was fully entitled to make.'

How Do They Do That? was not, most observers feel, a ratings winner. Des, who was optimistic about the show, clearly wasn't happy about its tone, or content towards the end of his second series. That, and the difficulties of finding any other television vehicle in which Des operates comfortably leads inevitably to speculation that Des should stick to what he knows best. But is that Des's fault? Or our own?

The fact that Des doesn't transplant well could be partly due to the fact that people feel more confident when they are on their own territory. Sport is what he really knows and where he is most respected by other people. Take him out of that environment and, maybe, his uncertainties seep through.

Perhaps, though, this perception that Des the chat show host is not as good as Des the sports presenter is something that we project on him. He would certainly be sensitive enough to pick up on anything like that and, perhaps, feel that something wasn't working quite as well as it should.

Secretly, we don't want to see Des out of his slot. When we see him we immediately connect him with sport and, to some degree, we are disappointed when the connection is not sport. To that extent, he suffers from typecasting in the same way as the star of a long-running soap opera.

Des, who is a deep thinker, constantly analyses his own performances and agonizes over any apparent fault. He's not happy if he perceives anything less than the best.

He says:

'It is a strange way to make your living, sitting there for hours on end, talking to people you can't see. What are the pleasures of it . . . ? Getting it right, I suppose. People think that what you enjoy is having your face up there on the screen, but I would claim that wasn't the case for me. I'm actually quite shy about that. For me the actual process of doing live television, the studio with all its technical bits and pieces, is a limited pleasure. The real pleasure comes afterwards. The feeling of having got through, of it having gone all right.'

Des is constantly aware of his responsibilities to the people watching at home, and of the bigger events, the broader picture. He constantly puts his own sporting world into the context of the wider world outside.

He adds:

'I am fully aware of what sport can mean to people, those who watch it and those who play it. But I think you need to have a sense of scale. I found the Gulf War very, very difficult for instance. There were all these extra news bulletins during *Grandstand* and you would come back from some awful report and be expected to introduce some jolly old Rugby League or something. I had to be hauled back a couple of times by the editor for commenting on the incongruity of it all. My whole approach is based on the idea that, in the end, it's only sport.'

After his own flirtations with hosting a chat show, it must have been with a fair degree of trepidation that Des agreed to appear on the *Mrs Merton Show* in what became one of the highlights of a fabulously funny BBC series, just before Christmas in 1995. Mrs Merton, of course, is the cantankerous, grey-haired, old lady chat show host, an hilarious incarnation of comedienne Caroline Aherne. Her sharp wit and acid tongue guarantee a giggle for the studio audience and the folks at home but, by God, the guests aren't half nervous. She outpointed then verbally knocked out boxer Chris Eubank in one classic encounter and when she meanders off on some little anecdote, you just know there's an ambush waiting.

So, how would Des, whose own intellect and quick humour are the tools of his trade, fare against the 'harmless little old lady'. Her first guest that night had been nightclub owner Peter Stringfellow, whom Mrs Merton put away with a reference to his 'Second Division footballers' hairdo . . .'

Then she introduced Des with the build-up: 'My next guest has been voted the world's sexiest man for the last four years . . . by me and my friend Lily. Welcome, the dreamboat that is Desmond Lynam.' Des, romantically carrying a single red rose for Mrs M, quite easily sidestepped the first bullet, 'you've got charm oozing from every orifice' by responding with a smile, 'I've been working on it for about twenty-eight years.' He conceded, 'I have this slight reputation with women of a certain age.'

That was Mrs M's cue for a quote which will be repeated for ever more: 'Des, you are the Tom Cruise for menopausal women. We are putty in your hands, we really are.'

Mrs Merton's chats are like no other, however, and after meandering around with discomfiting questions about Des's bowel movements, she moved onto his brief hosting of the *Holiday* programme. 'What do you look like in trunks, Des?' she enquired. 'A bit dodgy around the leg area,' he replied. 'They could do with a bit more muscle tone.'

After the questions about whether or not he was regular, it looked as though Mrs Merton finally had Des on the ropes. He was smiling, but looking a little flustered. But he wasn't beaten yet. What would Des consider a romantic evening, wondered Mrs M. No problem. That was like a defence-splitting pass for our Des.

'A moonlit supper on the banks of the River Thames,' replied Des. 'I would get to know her mind . . . what makes her such a beautiful woman . . .' Then, having sent the keeper the wrong way with a neat bodyswerve, he quickly added: 'Do you want me to be honest now . . . ? Two pints of lager and then back to her place . . .'

When Mrs Merton sneaked a crafty kiss, the audience –

mainly consisting of ladies of a certain age – loved it. They reckoned the result was a rib-tickling draw and Des was drowned in a cacophony of cheers. He certainly came out ahead on points over Mrs Merton's next guest that night, the Australian entertainer Rolf Harris. 'Now tell me Rolf,' said Mrs Merton eventually. 'This is something I've always wanted to know . . . Why did you tie that kangaroo down . . . ?' As Rolf found out, there's no answer to that.

So, there's Des the entertainer, giving as good as he gets in a verbal swordfight with another rapier-like wit. But there is another, deeply thoughtful side to Des which comes out in his love of poetry. He has had an abiding interest in poetry since his schooldays. There was a famous occasion on *Match of the Day* when he wrote a link entirely from Shakespeare plays after hearing that one of the players on the show that day had been to drama school. And his end-piece in the 1998 World Cup was an inspired reading of Rudyard Kipling's 'If', set to a dramatic patchwork of film clips from the event, catching the heartbreaking moments and heart-stopping action.

When it went out, the BBC was inundated with requests from viewers who wanted to see it again, or wondering if they could get hold of a copy of Des reading the poem. It encouraged Des to release his reading of the poem as a single, accompanied by the BBC World Cup theme tune, Fauré's *Pavane*. But, more significantly, it led him to record an album of poetry readings featuring twenty-two of his favourites with a full orchestral accompaniment.

Called *Time to Stand and Stare*, the album has beautiful poems by Sir John Betjeman, Kipling, Roald Dahl and W.H. Auden. It also contains one by Des himself, 'The Silly Isles', which he wrote in 1982 as a kind of protest about the Falklands War.

Des says:

'I wrote it at Christmas in 1982 when I was on holiday in Spain. It was something that I felt very strongly about and I was moved to write about. I thought things had become very gung-ho.

'I wouldn't want to demean the efforts of the British

servicemen – they did what they considered to be their duty. But I also felt for the Argentinians who were killed. They were a conscript army. Frightened young lads. I feel more could have been done to avoid that war.'

Des the deep and serious thinker is a side of the man we the public rarely get a chance to see. But his ex-wife, Susan, says: 'Des was certainly thoughtful. He has hidden depths. He used to enjoy writing poetry – not for me, but it was something which interested him. He wrote quite a lot when his mother died. That affected him deeply.'

Des would ideally love to write side-splitting comedies but he has no delusions about his skills either as poet or comedian. He says: 'It's like the drummer wanting to play the trumpet, that sort of thing. I wrote a few other poems around the same time as "The Silly Isles" but since then I haven't really written anything. But I love poetry deeply and I was very glad to record the album. I don't have delusions of adequacy about it, even. It was the producer's idea to include "The Silly Isles" on the album.'

The album was produced by Mike Cobb from BBC Music. He says: 'It was not a gimmick. The sentiment comes from Des's heart – he reads beautifully. A lot of commercial poetry readings are done by actors and they do it very well, perhaps too well. With Des you get a sincerity and a familiarity which makes all of the recordings seem extremely immediate.'

Recording was done over a period of six weeks but Mike Cobb pays full tribute to Des's professionalism. He adds: 'Des never needed more than two takes to get a poem on tape, which is remarkable. He is a very modest man. His own poem, "The Silly Isles", was something I pushed him into recording. It's a very moving piece.'

Des's selection of poems for *Time To Stand and Stare* reveals a melancholic streak. Maybe, even, a fascination with death. There's Betjeman's 'On a Portrait of a Deaf Man' which carries the line: 'He looked so wise but now I do not like to think of maggots in his eyes.' While a line from a Roger McGough poem reads: 'Every day I think about dying.'

But Des says the selection is meant to be thought-provoking and stimulating. He says: 'I guess there is a melancholic side to me otherwise I wouldn't like these poems or be able to read them. But I'm certainly not prone to depression. The glums now and again, like everyone else, sure. Good days and bad. But generally my spirits are sailing high. On an even keel. Emotionally steady.'

This aspect of Des is just one of the many apparent contradictions which add up to his overall character, his individuality. That extra spark which sets him apart from other first-class broadcasters. His childhood shyness is an indication of his thoughtful and intelligent nature. Even the subjects he was good at at school – French, Art, English – are quite introverted subjects.

And then what does this shy, introverted, intelligent person do – give up a safe, steady job in insurance to pursue his hobby – broadcasting. Like many, I originally felt that the two worlds of insurance and broadcasting must be at opposite ends of the universe, as far as the personality traits required for success in either are concerned. But, in actual fact, the more you think about it, the more you can see how Des's years in insurance were perfect preparation for the career to come.

He had already broken the shackles of his shyness by entering a profession where you need to develop your extrovert characteristics in order to sell. Selling is not for the faint-hearted or those who cannot sell themselves. As an agent for Cornhill, Des would have had to develop that capacity to be able to communicate with other people and sell them ideas and concepts.

In a way it secured for him the ideal balance of personality traits – someone who is both thoughtful and intelligent, yet capable of communicating clearly and with persuasion. You have to sell yourself to sell insurance, so Des's show business personality was almost certainly cut in selling insurance.

As a broadcaster, Des has to come across as a sort of powerful, charismatic, persuasive person. He could, if the mood had taken him, even have gone into politics where exactly the same personality characteristics are required. Millions of sports fans are glad that Des felt that there was something missing from his life as he toured the farms, factories and offices of East Sussex for Cornhill. We're glad he developed his hobby and brought his thoughtful approach to sports broadcasting.

As soon as he got his foot in the door, his rapid rise was assured. So what if he never quite became the next Robin Day, Michael Parkinson or Jeremy Paxman. As the great Liverpool manager Bill Shankly used to say: 'Football's not a matter of life or death. It's much more important than that.'

9

Ali and Me

'. . . one of the most moving images I have ever seen in my time in sports broadcasting.'
> – Des on Muhammad Ali carrying the
> Olympic torch in Atlanta

As the Swinging Sixties shimmied into the Psychedelic Seventies, Des Lynam had more to worry about than who was at the top of the musical charts. His contribution to the booming radio days concerned a very different kind of hit parade. As the BBC's latest radio boxing commentator he had some very big shoes to fill indeed – those of the legendary Eamonn Andrews who had moved onto bigger and brighter things after years bringing the ringside atmosphere from the world's biggest fights into living rooms around Britain.

This was an era when British beef was on a bone-shuddering high with the likes of John Conteh, Lloyd Honeyghan and Alan Minter disposing of all-comers on the world stage. Mixing it with the hard-nosed pack of journos and broadcasters who followed the fight game could have been unnerving for someone so relatively new to the broadcasting arena but, as was to become his trademark, Des fitted the pack as comfortably as their well-worn jackets. He had managed to do soccer reports and a little bit of boxing for Radio Brighton but it was when he graduated to national network radio that his chance to join the big hitters finally materialized.

'One day, this new face turned up at ringside doing the

boxing commentary and he became a regular fixture,' recalled journalist Colin Hart, who has covered boxing for British newspapers for more than forty years.

'I remember being in Belgrade with him when Conteh fought Matty Parlong and that was when he really became an accepted member of our little travelling group.

'He was really quite good at what he did. You know, you sit and listen to a guy asking questions and you soon know whether or not he's making a prat of himself by asking something stupid. But Des knew his business all right. He was obviously knowledgeable about boxing and he was immediately accepted by the boxing writers who wouldn't give tuppence for anyone who wasn't dedicated to and knowledgeable about the sport.'

Des enjoyed the camaraderie of boxing trips abroad – something that he would never have experienced as an insurance salesman no matter how high he had climbed through the Cornhill ranks.

'That night in Belgrade he came out with us for a meal and you could see straight away that he had the gift of the gab,' added Colin. 'We made him a member of the Boxing Writers' Club which he appreciated. Then, and on later trips, we would talk into the small hours, but although Des could hold the floor for ages he never talked about himself. I didn't know anything about his personal life and it appears he has always preferred it that way. He was always very good company and very amusing, though.'

Just how Des gained his impressive boxing knowledge is a bit of a mystery. Arthur Smith recalls Des saying he had boxed a bit himself as a youngster. Tall and quite skinny, he would probably have made an awkward opponent, but certainly the idea of being punched for a living didn't appeal to Des – whether he was any good at it or not. Writing about boxing – and better still, reporting live from ringside for an eager radio audience – was an altogether more attractive way to be involved in the sport.

Des has often remarked that the greatest sporting spectacle he has ever seen involved his hero, Muhammad Ali. The day his beloved Brighton and Hove Albion made it to the FA Cup Final against Manchester United comes a close second, and is probably his favourite soccer moment even though Brighton lost. But, for Des, nothing could top the events of 1974.

1974 was the year of the great Rumble in the Jungle – probably the most famous fight in boxing history, when Muhammad Ali took on the mighty George Foreman in the steamy heat of Zaire which was formerly the Belgian Congo. The Government of Zaire wanted to put their new nation firmly on the world map and with the aid of a newly-emerging boxing force called Don King they pulled off the most spectacular public relations coup imaginable.

It was the fight the whole world wanted to see. It had everything – glamour, spectacle, unique location and, of course, two of the best heavyweights ever to climb through the ropes of a boxing ring. Ali himself loved the deal. He had already turned his back on the name with which he became an Olympic champion, Cassius Clay, saying that was his 'slave name'. Now here he was, returning to what he believed to be his spiritual homeland – the land from which so many slaves were taken in less enlightened times. The hyped-up heavyweight battles of later years could never even come close to the drama and magic that was created around this one fight.

By now firmly established at the BBC, Des Lynam was one of the millions eagerly anticipating the clash of the Titans, but as a boxing correspondent he had an ace up his sleeve – he would be one of the chosen few to view the fight from ringside.

The boxing press flew out to Kinshasa as Rumble-in-the-Jungle-fever swept the world. Immediately upon arrival in the vast Central African state they were taken to Nsele, a complex of 'luxury' huts built by the Chinese for President Mobutu to entertain visiting VIPs and currently doubling as the training camps for Foreman and Ali.

The high spirits, however, were soon dashed when one of the American press corps who had been there several days already, shouted across, 'The fight's off, fellas,' as they disembarked from their transport. It was to be the start of a nightmare of frustrating delays which would see the fight put back for more than six weeks. Foreman, it was said, had been cut in training and it was going to take six weeks for him to heal.

Initially the hacks busied themselves filing 'colour' pieces, relaying the atmosphere and the exotic flavours of the old Congo. There were regular updates from both camps: how well Foreman was responding to treatment; the latest outrages from the Louisville Lip who was notorious for his extravagant statements. Ali once famously said of Foreman: 'I've seen him shadow boxing . . . and the shadow won.'

Of another world class heavyweight with whom he had some major battles, Ali quipped: 'Joe Frazier's so ugly they ought to donate his face to the World Wildlife Fund.' And regarding Sonny Liston, from whom he first took the world title, Ali jabbed: 'He's so ugly that when he cries the tears run down the back of his neck. He's too ugly to be world champion. The world champion should be pretty . . . like me.'

He stopped at nothing to entertain the paying public and on those long, hot, sweat-stained days in Zaire, with nothing much happening, any pronouncements from the Ali camp were seized upon like juicy bones thrown to starving wolves.

Amidst it all, the one man more frustrated than either boxer was Des Lynam. And he eventually blew his top. Though the Zairean authorities were doing their best to be good hosts, there was chaos in the area most important to the whole exercise – communication. Getting a phone call out of the country was a virtual impossibility. Transmitting a radio report back to Broadcasting House was about as likely as Ali becoming modest. It just couldn't happen.

'The press boys were wiring their stuff back to their newspapers, but poor old Des just could not get one phone call through to do his radio stuff,' recalled Hart. 'The so-called laid-back Lynam was shouting and cursing and carrying on at the authorities because he could not do his job. If the millions who regard him as the most laid-back personality in Britain could have seen him then they would have been amazed.

'He was effin' and blindin' like a good 'un.'

Eventually, after three weeks, the Zaire authorities allowed the foreign press to leave the country. They had tried to keep them in Kinshasa for the duration of the delay – just in case they lost interest and didn't return for the big fight. Some chance of that.

However, when the time came for the Rumble to go ahead and the corps reassembled, there was at least one notable absentee. Des's bosses at the BBC decided it was a pointless waste of time sending him back to Kinshasa, mainly because of the communication problems, and so Des missed one of the greatest occasions in the history of boxing. It is something he regrets to this day. Ali won the remarkable battle which went ahead in the middle of the night to catch American prime-time TV audiences, and no one who was there can recall a more incredible event.

Ali regained the world heavyweight title which he had first claimed in 1964. His eighth round knockout in front of 60,000 fans – and millions more on television – made him only the second ever boxer to regain the world heavyweight title.

'The irony is,' recalled Hart, 'that there had been so many complaints that by the time we got back they had improved communications and everyone there was able to file the story or get their reports back with no problem.'

Legendary commentator Harry Carpenter might have wished that there had been a further hiccup during his own ringside transmission. With Foreman clearly getting the better of things inside the ring, as Ali operated what he termed his 'rope a dope' policy of soaking up everything the giant opponent could throw at him, Carpenter told the world, 'That's it. There's no way Ali can win this one now.' As gaffes go, Carpenter's prediction was a knockout. Within seconds, Ali had landed a stunning knockout punch of his own to end Foreman's title dream.

Forced to watch the drama unfold from a television set back in England, Des still reckons it was the greatest fight ever seen. 'Muhammed Ali regaining the world heavyweight title from George Foreman was the greatest spectacle I've ever seen in sport,' he says.

If Des has ever truly revered a sporting idol it has to be Ali. In 1998 he was delighted to be asked to front *Ali Night* for BBC2 – a whole evening of programming devoted to arguably the best heavyweight boxer ever. Not only did it mean an excuse to re-run footage of classic Ali fights, most of which Des would have watched from ringside, it also meant an opportunity for Des to travel across the States, meeting Ali's legendary cornerman Angelo Dundee, his former ringside doctor Ferdie Pacheco and Ali's brother Rahman Ali.

It was a labour of love.

Des recalls:

'In person Ali was remarkable. Even the most cynical hack would spend two minutes in his presence and end up in love with him. He was certainly the most charismatic sportsman I have ever met. He could stop the traffic in any country in the world, yet he always had time for people.

'And he was blessed in a physical sense – even his rounded facial features were perfect for boxing: punches just slid off him so he never got cut. And there wasn't a more courageous fighter, though sadly he paid a terrible price for that in the end.'

Along with Rahman Ali, Des re-visited the bridge in Louisville, Kentucky, where a young Cassius Clay, fresh from the Rome Olympics of 1960, threw his precious gold medal into the Ohio River after being refused service in a segregated restaurant. It's hard to imagine such prejudice against one of the world's greatest-ever sportsmen, but in those days, sadly, it was the norm in certain parts of the deep south. From that incident the seeds were sown which eventually saw Ali convert to Islam – not before, however, he had visited London in 1963 to fight Henry Cooper.

The extraordinary fight in which ' 'Enry's 'Ammer' became the punch that shook the world and almost changed boxing history took place at no less than Wembley Stadium. Cooper's famous left hook flattened young Cassius Clay but Angelo

Dundee, mysteriously, found a split in his fighter's glove which then had to be replaced – giving Clay valuable time to clear his senses and get back into the fight. It allowed him also to continue an unbeaten journey to the World Heavyweight Championship. But, oh, how much more difficult would it have been had he lost to the brave Briton.

The fight is another of Des's treasured boxing memories.

The pilgrimage also took Des to the gymnasium where 'the Greatest' began his legendary career. It all started when Cassius approached a policeman to complain that his bicycle had been stolen. The policeman turned out to be a boxing coach called Joe Martin and he persuaded the angry young man to vent his frustrations in the boxing ring.

One of Des's favourite Ali stories concerns a flight the great man and his entourage were making from Washington to New York. Ali, or the 'Louisville Lip' as he was sometimes known, was never willingly beaten to the punch or the punch line. But he more than met his match when a tiny air stewardess gave him a hard time for refusing to do up his seatbelt.

Staring her straight in the face, Ali said, 'Sister, Superman don't need no seatbelt.' But she was too quick for him and put him away with the knockout reply: 'Mister, Superman don't need no plane either.'

Des was able to pay further tribute to Ali when he presented a video compilation of some of boxing's greatest moments in the late 1990s. With Des's name and photograph in a suitable, two-fists raised, boxing pose figuring prominently on the cover it was sure to be a big seller and made it into the video top ten sales charts. The subtitle of the video was *Boxing: The Good, The Bad and The Ugly*.

It was something of a busman's holiday for Des as he took a mental stroll down memory lane to bring us clips from some of the boxing world's greatest ever fights. For the Good Guys of boxing, famed for their sublime skills, extraordinary balance and speed and accuracy in delivering a punch, Des picked out fighting greats like Joe Louis, the so-called 'Brown Bomber', Larry Holmes and Floyd Patterson and the two sensational Sugar Rays – Leonard and Robinson.

Recalling the funeral of Joe Louis, thought by many to be the best boxer ever, Des couldn't resist quoting his own favourite, Ali, who said, 'I just gave lip service to being the best. He *was* the best.'

Although with the evidence to hand in Des's own video, there are a number of candidates for that prestigious honour. Sugar Ray Robinson, points out Des, is often regarded as the best pound-for-pound fighter ever, and the tear-up between Sugar Ray Leonard and Thomas 'Hit Man' Hearns in 1981 is one of the all-time great boxing events. Leonard came back from a severe battering to stop Hearns who was way ahead on points.

Of boxing's Bad Guys – those who are ruthless finishers with concussive punching power – Des includes Britain's own 'Dark Destroyer' Nigel Benn in his selection. He pays tribute, though, to the best bruisers in history from Jack Dempsey in the 1920s to Gene Tunney and the 'Battle of the Long Count' in 1927 when Tunney went down for fourteen seconds because the referee refused to start the count until Dempsey had gone to a neutral corner. The fight should have been over, but Tunney recovered and won on points to end the great Dempsey era.

Then, amongst the Bad Guys, there was Rocky Marciano, one of the most intimidating heavyweights the world had ever seen, says Des, and Jersey Joe Walcott who threw the hardest punch ever in a world title fight in 1952. In more modern times there were 'marvellous' Marvin Hagler, Roberto Duran and our own Nigel Benn. Des says: 'His inclusion is a must. He was a true warrior with a big heart. A perfect illustration of boxing's Bad Guys, he was always out to nail his opponent.'

But the top of the Bad Guys league has to be 'Iron Mike' Tyson who fought his way out of the slums of New York to win the world heavyweight title from Trevor Birbick in 1986. Like a bull in a china shop, rampaging Tyson ravaged Birbick and then, in June 1998, he unified the heavyweight world with the total destruction of the other undefeated heavyweight champion, Michael Spinks, in justninety-one seconds.

Sadly, reflects Des, the great almost supernatural power that was Tyson then seemed set on a course of self-destruction. As his career spun out of control Tyson lost to Buster Douglas in

166

a fight he should never have lost, spent three years in jail on rape charges, and then secured his place in boxing's hall of infamy by biting part of Evander Holyfield's ear off during a title fight.

The 'Ugly' side of boxing, according to Des focuses on the controversies and even illegalities which have scarred the sport's long and illustrious history. Things like the fight when Jack Johnson lost his title in Havana, Cuba: though supposedly knocked out, he raised his hands to shield his eyes from the sun in the open air ring! And even the legendary Ali courted controversy. Ali beat Sonny Liston to win the world heavyweight title in 1964 even though Liston was 7-1 on favourite. In the rematch, as Ali defended his title, he won with what boxing aficionados always refer to as a 'phantom punch'. It is a much-studied incident still talked about more than thirty years on.

What cannot be denied is that Ali went on to become the most colourful personality the sport has ever known. Des describes Ali like this: 'He transcended sport to become the icon of the twentieth century – the most famous man in the whole world.'

Ali's great boast was: 'I float like a butterfly, sting like a bee. His hands can't hit what his eyes can't see.' In a rollercoaster of emotion and drama he took the world's boxing press – and broadcasters like Des – on a whirlwind ride through some of the most spectacular and sometimes bizarre nights in boxing history. A year after the famous Rumble in the Jungle in Zaire in 1974, he fought Joe Frazier in the Philippines in what Ali himself called 'The Thriller in Manila'. And thrilling it was. The fight is regarded by many as one of the greatest ever and it proved that Ali could be one of the toughest Bad Guys if necessary.

In tribute to Ali, Des says:

'I spent most of the 1970s and 1980s commentating on boxing for BBC radio. I had the pleasure of covering a great number of title fights and sharing the stories of a great era.

'There is absolutely no doubt in my mind that Muhammed Ali was the most extraordinary man I have ever met. I have interviewed him many times – although I never got to say much. As well as being brilliant in the ring he was also the great communicator and it breaks my heart to see that wonderful communicator almost silenced by illness.'

The dramatic moment when Ali, suffering from Parkinson's disease, carried the Olympic torch at the opening of the Games in Atlanta, almost moved Des to tears. He recalls: 'That is one of the most moving images that I have ever seen in my time in sports broadcasting.'

In the autumn of 1985, Des displayed a courageous talent for speaking his mind in difficult circumstances while skilfully bobbing and weaving around the dangers. In boxing terms it was the verbal equivalent of nifty footwork – a smile here and a raised eyebrow there standing in for a drop of the shoulder and a delicate feint while the knockout blow was being delivered.

A capacity, and typically enthusiastic, crowd at Belfast's King's Hall had just roared plucky little Barry McGuigan through the first successful defence of his WBA Featherweight title against dangerous American challenger Bernard Taylor. McGuigan, the new darling of British boxing fans, had won the title in June and, with a champion's right, elected to defend it in front of his fanatical home supporters.

After the fight, the McGuigan corner decamped to a luxurious hotel in Holywood, Co Down, not far from the home of McGuigan's mentor and fight promoter Barney Eastwood. It was a great occasion and Eastwood, a self-made millionaire bookmaker with a string of shops across Northern Ireland, was enjoying holding court. The boat had been well and truly pushed out as the assembled boxing writers and commentators indulged in Mr Eastwood's largesse. The celebratory atmosphere was intoxicating by itself.

It seemed as though the whole of Belfast had crammed into the restaurant – with the notable exception of the little fella himself. Boxer Barry hated the post-fight back slapping that these dos inevitably became.

As the evening progressed, Eastwood drew the attention of the room to make a speech, which some observers later described as 'very self-serving, self-congratulatory stuff'. He talked about the huge contracts with America which he had negotiated and how he was now a force to be recognized in the cut-throat world of boxing promotion. Several others made similar speeches, mainly about how well they had all done.

Suddenly Des, who had been commentating on the fight from ringside for the BBC, rose to his feet and cleared his throat. 'I'd just like to say that I am very pleased so many people in this room have done so well,' he intoned. 'But I'd also like to mention the name of a little man who is the reason we are all here tonight and whose name has not so far been mentioned. And *his* name is Barry McGuigan.'

One of the assembled Press corps recalls:

'There was a silence – a brief but stunned silence. And then everyone applauded. McGuigan never went to these dinners and his name had not been mentioned by any of the speakers. They owed it all to him but weren't giving him any of the credit. If someone had walked in from Mars and said, "Why are all these people gathered here tonight?" they would have thought we were there to celebrate Barney Eastwood, not Barry McGuigan.

'Des nailed that with a typically apt remark. Eastwood kept the smile on his face but no one missed the significance. In fact, one or two of us felt a little guilty because we were enjoying ourselves and yet we owed it all to McGuigan and we had barely noticed that he wasn't there. Afterwards I was told that Eastwood was pretty cross with Des and that he had 'stuck his neck out' by speaking up, especially as he was a top table guest. Eastwood was a very powerful man.

'Certainly, if he had wanted, Barney could have squeezed the BBC out of any TV deals for forthcoming fights just because he had fallen out with someone. Des would have known the politics behind the scenes but he was not afraid to speak his mind. Everyone agreed that

Des had been brave in standing up like that. Barney took no lasting offence, though, and I saw him and Des chatting happily on subsequent occasions.'

Barry McGuigan remains one of the UK's best-loved fighters. His plucky displays and superb skills always guaranteed a massive audience and a hugely entertaining fight night. He became a world favourite as well as a world champion and when, on one famous occasion, his father sang 'Danny Boy' in the ring before a fight, there wasn't a dry eye in the house.

Barry is a great fan of the man with the mike, though. Des the radio commentator as he was when Barry first met him. He recalls:

'Des has done all my fights and has been a great influence.

'My first international amateur success, I'll never forget it, he was working for BBC radio over in Edmonton, Canada, in 1978. He was doing the radio commentary and he called the fight an awful lot better than Harry Carpenter did. He thought I had won and Harry, on TV, said he thought the other guy had been robbed.

'Well, at least he thought I had been beaten, whereas Des read it better. It was a much closer fight than I wanted but I won it – I knew that in my heart and Des knew that too. I remember thinking, at least this guy has done me a favour. He knows his boxing.

'He was there on all my big nights. The night I won the title he presented the show from Queen's Park Rangers, with Alan Minter doing the colour and Harry Carpenter at the ringside. He actually commentated on one of my fights, against Valerio Nati when I won the European title.

'He was synonymous with the highlights of my career.

'Harry is a great commentator and a historic name and everything else, but Lynam was every bit as important to the show all the way through my career. Those were his embryonic stages in his TV career and he was already showing that he had a great future. Now ten to fifteen years later he has really blossomed.

'I meet him from time to time and he comes along and supports various things I do. He had a great background in boxing. He had obviously read a lot about it and studied it. You need that if you are going to call a fight well.'

Barry went on to carve a new career in television for himself after he hung up his gloves. He adds:

'Des is probably the most charismatic figure in TV at the moment. Everyone looks up to him. He's the one everyone aspires to being and he's a great example to everybody.

'In many ways I have learnt a lot from him over the years – his equanimity, his calmness. He does everything with such aplomb. He's just such a professional, you know.

'He makes it look easy. When everything is going mad around him, he looks calm. He's like a swan on the water, you know – the feet are going like crazy beneath the surface but on top everything looks calm and relaxed.

'He has been an example to so many young presenters. He's the best around and he's a gentleman too. He's a lovely fella and I'm proud to say he's a friend of mine.'

Another boxer who has been a friend of Des for almost thirty years is the former World Middleweight Champion Alan Minter. Minter had a distinguished career which Des followed with great delight and the pair have remained friends even after Minter's retirement from the ring.

Minter recalls: 'Des has been a great mate. I have stayed at his house a few times when we have been to events and awards ceremonies in London and he has always been very good to me.'

Minter first met Des at the Munich Olympics in 1972. A good middleweight prospect at the time, twenty-one-year-old Minter won a bronze medal, although he always insists he was robbed of a chance of a glorious gold by 'disgraceful political judging' when he fought a German in the semi-finals.

Nicknamed 'Boom Boom', Minter turned professional after the Olympics but it was three years before he made a significant impact on the boxing world. In 1975 he outpointed Kevin Finnegan to become British Middleweight Champion. It was a 15-round 'war', as was the return which Minter also narrowly won a year later.

Minter was a 'southpaw', which means he leads with his right fist rather than his left like the majority of boxers. It can make them trickier to fight because their style is so obviously different from that which a boxer normally prepares against. He eventually got a crack at North American Champion 'Sugar Ray' Seales, who said: 'I'm going to rough up, mess up, cut up Minter. He's in trouble.'

That sort of hype angered Minter who said: 'That sort of rubbish gets right up my nose. I've never been hurt by hard words or dirty looks.'

He dropped Seales in the fifth round with the best right-hand punch of his career and went on to win the European Championship against the Italian Germano Valsecchi in Milan in 1976. When he woke up later, Valsecchi said, 'I have never been hit and hurt so much in my life.'

The ups and downs of a fighter's career continued when Minter lost to Marseille fighter Gratien Tonna because of cuts in 1977 which cost him his European title. Then he had to fight Kevin Finnegan again to win back his British title, which had been taken away because of Minter's European commitments.

With Des at the ringside for many of Minter's classic fights, he battled back to regain his European title against Angelo Jacopucci, who was knocked unconscious in the twelfth round but, sadly, later died in hospital. Tragedies in the ring are, thankfully, rare but they do happen from time to time. The death of a fellow fighter always affects a boxer badly, and Minter needed plenty of reassurance and support from those close to him, including Des, after Jacopucci's death.

With a true fighter's courage, Minter put behind him the tragedy of Jacopucci and the bitterness of his own past struggles and disappointments to climb back to the highest heights – a challenge for the world title.

It was two years later and Vito Antuofermo was the undisputed Middleweight Champion of the World. Minter climbed through the ropes determined to lift the belt for Britain and after an amazingly tough battle he got it by the narrowest of margins. He was actually awarded the fight on the decision of the English judge after the other two judges had marked it all square, so there was a touch of controversy surrounding the greatest win of his career so far. There was no controversy about the result of the return fight which took place in London, though. Minter stopped Antuofermo in eight one-sided rounds to prove beyond doubt that he was the best in the world at that time.

But boxing is no respecter of champions, not a sport where a winner can sit back on his laurels and enjoy the view from the top. Just three months later Minter fought the brilliant American bruiser Marvin Hagler and suffered mercilessly. In the end, the fight was stopped in the third round because Minter's face became so badly cut. It was the beginning of the end for one of Britain's bravest champions. A short time later he lost his European title to Tony Sibson, another great Briton, and a fine career came to a close.

Des's affection for boxing and boxing people is not related to how well they're doing at the time. He has as much respect for any fighter who is prepared to climb through the ropes and put himself on the line as he has for those who reach the very top. In a world where friends multiply faster than a Bill Gates computer during the good times, but vanish like the ice in your drink when the good times are gone, Des has always been regarded as a man who sticks by his mates.

'He's good company and a good friend,' adds Minter. 'He's a knockout.'

Boxing is one of the three sports Des will never tire of – the others being football and tennis. He doesn't, personally, have a great deal of time for sports like squash or basketball or rowing either as a viewer or a participant. His own mainstay of exercise, apart from regular sessions of his beloved tennis is a daily routine of T'ai chi, the ancient Chinese exercise. He always does twenty minutes of T'ai chi as part of his daily morning routine.

Would he have liked to have been a boxer if life had dealt the cards differently?

Not according to Minter. 'He has too much respect for those who do climb into the ring to imagine that it's easy,' says the former champ.

10

Brighton Forever

'If you mention Des Lynam, most football fans will know
he supports Brighton.'
                    – Tim Carder, Albion Supporters' Club

Supporting your local football team can mean a roller-coaster
ride through the emotions as the ups and downs of soccer life
result in sometimes dramatic swings of fortune. Nowhere,
perhaps, have those mixed fortunes of football been more
keenly felt than at Brighton and Hove Albion – the team
supported since childhood by Des Lynam.

As a boy, then as a young man, he was proud to stand on the
terraces at Goldstone, cheering the 'Seagulls' come rain or
shine, hell or high water. He was, and is, by his own admission
'an ardent fan'. Even before he began his career in broadcasting,
writing reports about minor league football and then filing
reports for Radio Brighton from wet and windy Sussex
grounds, you can imagine Des playing over in his mind a kind
of running commentary as each Brighton game commenced. It's
the kind of thing most young sports fans do at some time or
another.

'Grealish wins the ball in midfield. He passes to Case who
slides the ball through to Lynam. Lynam beats one, beats two
. . . he shoots . . . goooooaaaalllll. Lynam wins the FA Cup for
Brighton . . .' As Des quipped at the opening of Euro 96 . . .
'Well, we can dream, can't we?'

Maybe, even then, as a passionate young Seagulls fan, he

dreamt of emulating the great commentators of the day not real-izing that he would, in fact, eclipse them all as a broadcaster.

Certainly his loyalty to the club would eventually be sorely tested – as it would for all the Brighton and Hove Albion fans. Over the seasons of bitter disappointment, through the traumas of relegation and behind-the-scenes boardroom battles, through the eventual loss and redevelopment of their ground and the near extinction of the club, thousands of Brighton fans would desert the Seagulls.

Des would not be among them. As one of a small but highly respected clique of celebrity fans who include actor Jamie Theakston, former England manager Ron Greenwood, ex-Olympic athlete Sally Gunnell and the legendary comic actor Norman Wisdom, Des kept faith with his local team. Stuck by them through thick and thin. Helped out in times of need. And as the club approaches its centenary in 2001, he is still there, encouraging from the sidelines, getting involved where neces-sary, and generally exhibiting the colours of a true fan as, finally, Brighton and Hove Albion begin to put the past troubles behind them and build a bright new future.

This is one of the reasons Des can so easily reach out to foot-ball fans from the comfort zone of the BBC studios; why he can accurately gauge the feeling and deliver the right reaction in times of triumph or turmoil; and why his sharp wit finds such a deep-seated target in the psyche of those who follow football, through all its ups and downs, in Britain.

Des Lynam was an ordinary fan. The Goldstone ground, which has since been knocked down and re-developed as a retail park featuring the usual suspects of Toys'R'Us, Comet and a DFS furniture store amongst others, was one of those special places only football fans would take to their hearts. It had a north stand, full of atmosphere, where young Des stood and watched his team from the terraces before moving to the long stand full of seats as he grew older. Finally, as he became a celebrity, it would be the directors' box, where the great and the good were invited to sit.

Opposite the directors' stand was one of those quirky arrangements which gave a ground like the Goldstone its character. The houses behind that terracing were afforded a superb view of the pitch and the sight of people standing in gardens watching the game was a common enough one. Later, when the club's troubles spilled over into acrimony between fans and directors, some of the more active fans found themselves banned from the ground – but still able to watch from the gardens next door.

Oddly, Des didn't see a game on his first ever visit to the ground. The opportunity arose when Des was ten years old and a neighbour invited him along to a match with his own two daughters one Saturday afternoon. It was in the days of old leather footballs that became more like cannonballs when they got wet. During the pre-match kick-about, one of the players sent the ball flying into the crowd and it caught one of Des's little friends squarely in the face, knocking her unconscious. Des recalls: 'It was a St John's Ambulance job and we all had to leave. Never even saw the game.' Over a drink or two, he often has pals in stitches by adding the punchline: 'It was my first experience of a woman's headache getting in the way of a lot of fun.'

'If you mention Des Lynam, most football fans will know that he supports Brighton,' says Tim Carder, chairman of the Albion Supporters' Club. 'He used to be a regular on the terraces. He doesn't go to see too many matches any more but his heart is there and whenever he is needed to assist with the numerous campaigns that we have had over the past few years, and which we will still need in the future until we once again have a permanent home of our own, Des is always there and willing to give whatever support he can.'

Everyone understands that Des has been unable to attend as many games as he would no doubt like ever since his career in sports broadcasting took off, but he has been vociferous in his support of the club in its recent misfortunes, just as he was a vocal fan when times were good. And for the Albion times were never better than in 1983 when for 120 glorious minutes they held out against the might of Manchester United before 92,000 enthralled fans in the FA Cup Final at Wembley. It must be said that, all in all, it was a bitter-sweet season for Brighton as they suffered the despair of relegation. But for the fans, those ninety minutes at Wembley, followed by extra time, were the sweetest memories of a sporting lifetime.

Des has seen it all: World Cup Finals, Olympic triumphs, epic centre court battles at Wimbledon between John McEnroe and Jimmy Connors. But Brighton's FA Cup Final appearance against Manchester United in May 1983 ranks among his favourite sporting moments.

United were huge favourites to lift the cup against the struggling seasiders, who were without their talismanic skipper Steve Foster whose suspension from the game remained in force despite a desperate last-minute court battle to get the ban overruled. Their side was bristling with international players like Ray Wilkins, Bryan Robson, Gordon McQueen, Frank Stapleton, Arnold Muhren and Norman Whiteside. But etched on Des's heart will be the names of the Brighton side who fought like lions: Graham Moseley, Chris Ramsay, Graham Pearce, captain Tony Grealish, Gary Stevens, Steve Gatting, Jimmy Case, Gary Howlett, Michael Robinson, Gordon Smith, Neil Smillie and substitute Gerry Ryan.

When the Wembley roar signalled the start of the match, the Albion fans were in good heart. They were ecstatic just thirteen minutes into the game when Gordon Smith's header beat Gary Bailey in the United goal to give Albion the lead.

Somewhere within the vast concrete edifice that is Wembley Stadium, Des's cries of delight almost raised the roof along with the thousands of other frenzied voices pitched high with joyous rapture.

Brighton were playing above themselves but when Frank Stapleton equalized for United early in the second half, followed by a terrific strike from England midfielder Ray Wilkins to make it 2–1 to United, hearts began to sink. Six minutes from full time, however, Gary Stevens fired the ball into the net for Brighton to take the game to 2–2. The frantic pace of the game continued through extra time and the Albion fans had their hearts in their mouths when Michael Robinson shrugged off the attentions of United's Kevin Moran and passed to the unmarked Gordon Smith just seconds from the final whistle.

Brighton fans will tell you he should have scored, while United's faithful point to an excellent save by Gary Bailey. Whatever, it meant a golden opportunity to lift the cup had slipped from their grasp. The replay on Thursday, 26 May, never lived up to expectation for the Brighton fans and United won comfortably 4–0, with two goals from Bryan Robson and one apiece from Norman Whiteside and Arnold Muhren.

Des said later: 'That FA Cup Final was one of the best games I have ever watched simply because my team were involved. That means you get more involved too. There was plenty of excitement . . . and we almost won.'

The following day some 40,000 fans braved appalling weather to welcome home the Brighton heroes but that heady few days left the club with a dreadful hangover which culminated in a spiral into first mediocrity, then farce. The old First Division crowds of 25-30,000 dwindled as the club fought for results in the Second. An expensive squad of highly-paid players could not be maintained and debts mounted. There were more seasons of heartbreak ahead. Play-off chances for promotion wasted, relegation battles looming, cash rows, managers sacked, directors booed and escorted from the ground for their own safety. By the end of 1992, Brighton and Hove Albion, one of the stalwarts of league football, faced a winding up petition in the High Court.

In the spring of 1993 Des was stung into action. On the eve of a High Court hearing which could have finished the club, goalkeeper Mark Beeney was sold to Leeds United, whose manager Howard Wilkinson had been a Brighton player, for £350,000. The bank draft was rushed to the Inland Revenue offices in Worthing to stave off the immediate danger. In the annals of Brighton and Hove Albion FC it has gone down as the greatest save by a goalkeeper in the history of the club.

It was obvious urgent action needed to be taken. Des quickly launched an SOS – Save Our Seagulls – campaign to prevent an untimely end for the cash-strapped club. His marathon broadcast in conjunction with Southern FM radio on 25 April 1993 has also been chronicled in the Seagulls' official history books. Ordinary supporters responded magnificently, raising more than £30,000 in a short space of time. But the lack of support from the local councils of the only club in the football league to straddle two neighbouring towns, clearly angered him. He told local campaigners he was very disappointed that Brighton Council hadn't got fully behind the club, but of the neighbouring town of Hove, he said witheringly: 'With the notable exception of one councillor, Hove Council have not helped the club, although it's interesting to note that its members were quite high on the list when the Cup Final tickets were being handed out.'

He was clearly pained by the club's predicament but he said: 'I have to earn a living and I don't have the time to take over the responsibilities of being the entrepreneur who fixes Albion. I didn't set a target for the SOS appeal but the local people were majestic. My aim was to make sure there was a football club left to save, because if it goes out of business that's the end.'

Tim Carder, chairman of the Supporters Club, says: 'The 1992–93 season was one of the most traumatic ever witnessed by supporters. Save Our Seagulls was Des's baby and it came at a crucial time when we were in trouble at the High Court. Des doesn't live here any more but he has done a lot to lift the profile of the club nationally. He does what he can, as all Albion supporters do what they can to help the cause.'

The club had debts of more than £4 million and a long saga of recriminations and counter-claims began between board members and supporters. By 1995 the board, headed by Bill Archer and Greg Stanley who bought all the shares in the debt-ridden club for £100, were threatening to sell the ground to pay off the club's debts and they did eventually sell it to a development group, with the football club allowed a year-long lease to continue playing there.

At this stage the prolonged in-fighting became very political and nasty. Some fans were banned from the ground, others claimed the club had been sold down the river for a quick profit and, eventually, the team's last home game of the 1996 season had to be abandoned when fans invaded the pitch and started a near riot in protest at what had been going on behind the scenes.

Paul Samrah, an accountant at the heart of the fans' battle to save the Goldstone ground, recognizes the contribution Des has made over the years but remains slightly critical that Des, apparently, kept his head below the parapet as the flak was flying and the ground was sold.

He says:

'Des is still liked and respected here but a lot of people were saying where is he when we need him – whether they were justified or not. He may have had strong views that he couldn't express because of his position at the BBC, but we would just have liked a message of support or at least he could have returned my calls. There are a lot of celebrity fans currently going round the circuit who put their heads above the parapet when it's easy to do so, or at least *easier* to do so.

'When all this blew up about three or four years ago, I rang Des at Television Centre and we had a chat. He was about to go off to the European Athletic Championships but he was keen to get involved in any way that he could, and he wanted to be kept informed of progress. But I was quite disappointed because he did not return my calls afterwards when he got back from the European Championships. I made contact again, updating him on the situation and I sent him a couple of letters but I did not have a response at all. Whether it was because he was under pressure from the BBC not to get involved or what-ever I don't know. I just thought he's a celebrity supporter and he's keeping a low profile.

'I don't wish to be over-critical but at the same time we needed friends at that particular time. We were knocking on doors at the FA, we were doing petitions, we were doing everything and our club was virtually on the point of extinction. We were a sensible group of people, you know, we weren't football nutters and we do have a life outside football but we were doing our best for the club. We were part of the mediation process that was going on but we didn't get a call from Des to ask how things were going.

'It was as though he was a fan, but he kept well away, didn't get involved at all, and we were going to Hell. Now we are going back to Brighton and he has appeared again.'

Other fans think that is a little harsh. During the crisis, as matters worsened, Des even phoned David Mellor's radio phone-in show and offered to act as a mediator between club chairman Archer and the angry fans. He said, 'Perhaps we could all get in a room and I could kick their backsides for a few hours and see if we could get something sorted out. Right now things are looking so black the club is going to die on its feet.' He also spoke out against plans to move the team away from Brighton and give them temporary accommodation sharing with Portsmouth. The plan would have seen Brighton play at Fratton Park in Portsmouth for three years while a new ground was built, but in a moving appeal he said, 'The thought of Albion moving to Fratton Park with no concrete plans to return to a new stadium fills me with horror. It would be the end of the road. If Albion is allowed to die it will be like cutting off this town's arm. A conurbation the size of Brighton and Hove must have a football stadium. If I had millions I would buy the club tomorrow and run it myself.'

He was invited to join the board, but he was smart enough to decline. He says: 'I knew they were trying to make me some sort of frontman so they could make some unpopular decisions and get me to explain them to the fans. I saw that one coming.'

Des urged the local councils to intervene, saying, 'I'm sure neither council wants Albion to die, but they have to be pro-active in saving it.' Calling on his vast knowledge of world football, Des pointed out that in Italy the local government of Milan had built a magnificent community stadium, the San Siro, and leased it to the city's two clubs AC and Inter Milan. With typical insouciance, he said, 'My call to the councils is simple: Follow Milan. They haven't done so bad.'

Eventually, however, the team were forced to play their home games at Gillingham – seventy-five miles and five motorways away as fans pointed out – as the Goldstone ground was finally demolished. In May 1999, the whole town was involved in a referendum aimed at agreeing a site for a super new £30 million stadium for the Albion – and Des was happy to lend his name in support of the scheme. He also became patron of the Albion's ladies' football section, aimed at encouraging more young girls to take up the game.

Says one fan, 'There's a limit to how much a man like Des can do. He has a high profile career and is obviously busy and we should all thank him for the assistance he has given to the cause over the years. When things were in complete turmoil, I'm not surprised he kept out of the way.'

Hove MP Ivor Caplin knows that Des's Brighton roots go deep. He says: 'Des has been a fan for many years and we have spoken about the Albion when times were dire. In 1995 in particular, when things were very bleak, Des would always encourage people to keep going, to keep fighting for the club.'

Mr Caplin was a local councillor when Des was urging the two authorities to step in and provide a lifeline for the club. But he says:

'Everyone who supported the club could never believe that someone would come along and sell the ground from under us. Proposals for the Council to buy the Goldstone ground were discussed at the time but the money that we were prepared to put on the table would have only covered the club's institutional debts. Much bigger sums were eventually involved. We put together a consortium in 1995/96 and the new board of Brighton is roughly that consortium.

'The supporters are absolutely first class down here and they have contributed hugely to the success we have had in keeping Albion going and now we have a secure future, something to build on. The club will be returning to Brighton to a temporary home at Withdean in July 1999 and exciting plans for a permanent sports complex which will benefit the whole area as well as become the new home of Albion are being considered.

'Des has not been to an Albion game for a while and I know his schedule would not allow him to take part as much as he would like to. But he has agreed to become patron of the women's football section, and that is one of the fastest growing areas of sport in the country. It is grass roots football in its widest sense.'

After enduring the exile of playing at Gillingham, Seagulls' fans finally began to see a possible end to their stormy seasons in the summer of 1999. And Des was one of those urging the towns-folk to grab the chance with both hands. The ambitious plan for a superb modern new stadium in the Falmer area between Brighton and Hove, and close to both fast road and rail links, was put to the people in the shape of a referendum. Some 83 per cent of those who voted urged the Council to ensure a future for Brighton and Hove Albion within the confines of the two towns, and 63 per cent voted in favour of the Falmer site.

Inevitably there was some degree of controversy. Would you want a major sports complex built close to your home? But the arguments of the pro-stadium lobby carried the day – at least as far as the public referendum was concerned. Securing planning approval may well be another matter, but the Brighton fans had at least won a major battle in their long campaign to preserve football for the town.

Des spoke out in support of the Falmer site plan and rein-forced his links with the club by supporting an event to launch the team's new sponsors and kit. Maybe it's appropriate consid-ering Brighton's troubled past, but the new sponsors for the 1999–2000 season turned out to be a company called Skint Records, whose figurehead is Norman Cook, aka Fatboy Slim, the pop star spouse of TV and radio celebrity Zoe Ball. To every-one's delight, Albion returned to the town for their 1999–2000 fixtures and the future seems more assured since approval for a new, permanent home was granted.

Des's home-town links have always been strong, even though he has now moved to a palatial beach-side residence further down the Sussex coast near East Preston. He and Rose spend as much time as possible there, away from his other luxury home on the Thames riverbank at Chiswick, London.

A few minutes' drive away is one of Des's favourite restaurants. He loves Thai food in particular and if he can enjoy the subtle tastes of the exotic cuisine in a quiet, out-of-the-way establishment without the hushed whispers and star-struck glances which are an appetite-quelling part of fame, then so much the better.

At Spices in Worthing he is always assured of a warm welcome from the staff, and the clientèle are unlikely to show too much interest in sharing their mealtimes with a celebrity. Even so, Des always asks for a corner table, out of the limelight, where he can tuck into his favourite dish of sizzling prawns and Siamese spring rolls, washed down with special Singha beer. He's a popular customer and, according to staff, a generous tipper!

His other favourite restaurant is also, surprise, surprise, Thai – a busy little place in Hammersmith in London, convenient for his Chiswick address.

But it's in the twin towns of Brighton and Hove where Des's appetite for success was nurtured. And where, in 1996, he almost saw the wheel of life turn full circle. Des fronted a £1-million bid to the Radio Authority from a consortium aiming to grab the licence for a new local radio station serving the towns. Franchises were offered for new stations throughout the country and the south coast area was seen as a prized catch after the BBC's Southern Counties Radio moved its headquarters to Guildford in Surrey.

Des wanted his Brighton FM station to return to local programming. It would have been an emotional return – even though he would have been on the periphery of day-to-day affairs – for the Silver Fox whose own fledgling career began in similar parochial style. Promoting his bid, Des said: 'I have great respect and admiration for regional radio stations, but I sometimes feel that some of the magic of truly local radio has disappeared.

'Brighton and Hove have got all the ingredients for a terrific, truly local station. We have articulate, individualistic people, a huge variety of life and many important local issues. I loved my days on Radio Brighton and I will always be grateful for the chance. I'd like Brighton FM to be able to do the same for other youngsters.'

Des has been involved in many projects away from his television role – not all of them runaway successes – but a return to his first love, local radio, would have been very close to his heart. Sadly it was not to be. Des's consortium lost out in the franchise battle to a commercial group, Surf 107, led by another broadcaster, Simon Fanshawe. Surf began broadcasting in 1997, but Des's hopes of contributing something to local radio, maybe after leaving his high profile television job, have certainly not been vanquished.

A local broadcaster who watched the developments keenly said:

'Des joined a group led by entrepreneur Rory McCloud, who started Southern Sound Radio down the coast, and who had a good track record in starting up new stations. They looked to have a strong hand and I remember Des took out ads in the local paper saying "Remember Radio Brighton" and saying how much he had enjoyed working on a truly local radio station. That was what he intended to bring back to the area.

'When they didn't win the franchise, I don't think they could believe it. The Radio Authority makes the choice on what they believe will be best for the area concerned. In this case they went with the commercial station headed up by Simon Fanshawe. I am sure Des and his group will just bide their time and try again if the franchise comes back on to the table.'

11

Catch of the Day

'I was with Des and Des is the man, you know. Des is the nuts, for want of a better word.'
– Ex-England international Ian Wright

It was, without doubt, the transfer coup of the summer. Arsenal had sold their disaffected player Nicolas Anelka to Italy for more than £23 million and spent most of the money on a host of big-name replacements. Manchester United were rattling the loose change in their deep pockets in the direction of Tottenham's £6 million-rated Darren Anderton, and Paul Ince had left Liverpool to join Middlesbrough for a snip at a mere £1 million.

But it was the deal struck in broadcasting's Premier League which shocked the whole of football, if not the whole of Britain, in the summer of 1999.

Des Lynam, the implacable face of BBC Sport, had moved across town to join their biggest rivals, ITV.

The significance of the event, and Des's place in our hearts, was amply illustrated by the acres of newspaper columns devoted to the surprising news. It became a major item on every television news bulletin on the night when reports of one of the world's worst train crashes were filtering through from India. And, in the aftermath, doom-mongers were playing the Requiem not just for BBC Sport but for the entire corporation.

Was the reaction justified? Certainly Des did not think so. He has always been aware of his power as a major national figure, but he has also been acutely aware of his limitations – the most galling of which was that his own bosses wouldn't listen to his pleas on behalf of BBC Sport. And, in the end, that was the reason he accepted the blandishments of ITV, not the fact that they were willing to pay him £1 million a year over the next four years.

Des had been with the BBC for thirty years but during the last ten he had seen live sports events haemorrhage away. Finally he risked becoming the emperor with no clothes.

As he bade farewell amidst all the razzamatazz of a big soccer signing, Des said:

'Leaving the BBC after thirty years was not an easy decision to make, but it was time for a new challenge and it is no secret that live football is what I loved. I do not wish to knock BBC Sport. They have done a marvellous job for me and I hope I have done a good job for them.'

He said he had become stale after the repetition of doing 'hundreds and hundreds of *Match of the Days* and Grand Nationals' and added: 'You have to ask yourself how you can freshen things up.

'It was a daunting decision but the offer was too good to refuse. I thought it would give me a shot in the arm and an injection of passion for it all again.'

Des explained his decision directly to Will Wyatt, chief executive of BBC Broadcasting, and revealed: 'He was particularly shocked about it because he wasn't expecting it. We talked about it in a gentlemanly way for about twenty minutes but I didn't give them a chance to make a counter offer. I had to make the decision.'

Des's loyalty to the BBC was legendary, but it had been sorely tested by his battles with corporation bosses over the love of his televisual life – sport in general and *Match of the Day* in particular. He turned down countless lucrative offers to leave the Beeb. BSkyB were ready to make him Britain's highest paid sports presenter and constantly courted him. But money was not Des's motivation. He has made himself a reasonably wealthy man on a BBC contract worth £500,000 a year and with other lucrative endorsements, but if money had been his *raison d'etre* he could easily have made himself a *very* wealthy man.

No, what irked Des more than anything is how the BBC had lost out in the competitive world of bidding for major events. In 1996, during the so-called Summer of Sport, Des was never off our screens. Not because of any ego trip, but because the BBC had three major events, – Euro 96, Wimbledon and the Atlanta Olympics – to present.

But the constant encroachment of BSkyB saw the satellite broadcaster win rights for live Premiership football, the Nationwide Football League, rugby union and rugby league; motor racing went to ITV and horse racing and cricket to Channel 4. And then, crucially, the rights to live England games also went to Sky and the greatest domestic prize of all, the FA Cup Final was snapped up by ITV.

Des's patience finally broke after the fledgling new Channel 5 secured rights to broadcast England's vital World Cup qualifying match against Poland in 1997. Having just signed a new contract with the BBC he expected a more robust approach in the bidding wars and said: 'This is not a good start. The people holding the purse strings at the BBC must be told that those millions who supported us through Euro 96 expect us to be in there trying to buy the best live football available.'

His stinging criticism drew support from the House of Commons Culture, Media and Sport Select Committee who accused Beeb bosses of 'throwing in the towel'. Tory MP David Faber said: 'Channel Four, to be blunt, stole cricket from under your noses. There is a view that the BBC has been lazy and arrogant. You have also lost the FA Cup Final at the time your presenter Des Lynam said the BBC should and could have found the money to keep it.'

Before Des's defection Eurosport executive Alan Hart, Des's former BBC boss, said:

'Des doesn't go around looking for ways to have little digs, he comes up front and says what he thinks and he has every right to say so if he thinks the BBC is losing its way.

'Des is as angry as anybody else in BBC Sport has been over the last few years. The BBC as an institution has not cared enough about sport over the last few years. In my day I had no problem getting the right support but I don't think that's necessarily the case today.

'I am sure Des has had some tempting offers. Sky would have loved to have got him, probably ITV have had a go too, but Des has remained loyal to the BBC. There are two ways of looking at it – what the BBC has lost or at what they still have. There is no *Match of the Day* on any other channel. There is no audience of that sort of size on a regular basis on any other channel.

'There is also the considerable portfolio of sport. You can't introduce the Grand National for instance on any other channel, the Olympic Games, Wimbledon etc. The portfolio may be less than it was but it is still formidable.'

Arthur Smith also observed Des's loyalty to the Beeb: 'Des is quite fiercely loyal but in his private moments he is quite down about what has happened at the BBC. He would have been hurt by the FA Cup loss and they didn't get England v Argentina in the World Cup and he was pretty pissed off about that. To me, it's at a moment like that that people want to watch BBC.'

Des's former colleague and rival Bob Wilson knows what a major blow losing the FA Cup Final was to the BBC sports team. He says:

'The fact that the FA Cup has now come to ITV as well as having the European Champions League vindicates my decision to move. Des was very upset. I think losing the FA Cup upset them more than anything else. I know they would love to be on the Champions League, too, but I don't see how the BBC can afford to compete for contracts like that. It's hard enough for ITV to bid for the Champions League, never mind the BBC.

'But the thing that upset Des most, and he spoke quite publicly about it, was the loss of the FA Cup.

'John Motson told me what an enormous blow it was to

lose the live coverage. The FA Cup Final day is a special day. There are few special events like Grand National day, the Wimbledon Final and the FA Cup Final.'

Gerry Williams, Des's 'double act' co-presenter of many years of Wimbledon tennis highlights, admitted:

'I left the BBC about five years ago to go to BSkyB and that was the end of Des and me at Wimbledon. I could see that on satellite TV we were going to do so much more tennis. It was a move that I had to make and I would make again.

'Also it's not a bad idea to stop something when you are winning. Some people go on and on and in the end they get kicked out.'

It wasn't that long ago that Des shouldered the responsibility of defending the BBC as the corporation came under attack for failing to bring the biggest sporting events into our homes. And once again, he wasn't reticent about voicing his thoughts strongly.

Phil Rostron, Sports Editor of the *Daily Star*, became more and more frustrated at what he perceived to be an erosion of a once-great BBC sporting service. Angrily he penned a back page leader branding the BBC as: Blind, Boring, Clueless. He says:

'That was back in 1993 – and look what's happened since. The situation has gone from bad to worse. When I had a go it was obviously only the thin end of the wedge. It was at the time Sky signed up rights to live Premiership soccer, European and League football had gone to ITV, ITV had signed up the rights to England's vital World Cup clash with Holland and the writing appeared to be on the wall for other sports and events, too.

'The feeling was that the BBC were failing more and more to compete for the big events and I felt that for the licence fee – at the time it was about £83 I think – people were entitled to expect a better service. A lot of our readers agreed with me. To his credit, Des stood firmly behind the BBC but I think the passage of time has proved me right.'

Des wrote an open letter to the *Daily Star* in which he pointed out that the BBC's deal for Premiership highlights – two featured games and the goals from every other match – was the best the BBC had ever had. Somewhat prophetically, however, he added that the BBC would have live FA Cup matches leading to exclusive coverage of the Final right up until 1997!

In a strong defence of the Beeb, he said:

'You say that ITV beat us to the Holland–England game. I can tell you that the BBC, with Sky, bid a great deal of money but were still pipped on price. I don't think I could convince your readers to pay double the licence fee. But if I could, then the BBC would be able to win all the battles.

'I will concede that the BBC could schedule some of its football coverage at a better time. But our football coverage remains a major priority within this organization. And with good reason. When *Match of the Day* returned last season, it arrived on a wave of enthusiasm and loyalty from our viewers.

'But the key thrust of your argument was that the BBC is "backing away from big-time sport". Nonsense. Where were you this summer? Where were the other broadcasters as a summer of spectacular sport unfolded on the BBC? Where did your readers watch Linford Christie, Sally Gunnell and Colin Jackson win World Championship gold?'

He went on to name several championship events to be seen on BBC and added that the BBC stood for the Biggest, the Best and the Choice of millions.

Unfortunately, if Des were to run through that list again as we head into the new millennium, he would find one or two significant omissions and that, if anything, was the key to him leaving.

Friends thought that Des would remain loyal to the BBC, in

spite of the disappointments and the obvious temptations of big money from BSkyB and ITV. They felt he would see out his contract which expired after the 2000 Olympics and would, maybe, hang on for the next World Cup. But with the 1999 domestic soccer season approaching he obviously looked again at the situation and began to wonder what was left in the locker. He had already dropped broad hints. After one particular approach by Sky he did admit: 'I thought about it very seriously. I was unhappy about the BBC's loss of product. The FA Cup Final in 1997 was our last for five years – and possibly for ever.'

Even so he remained as protective as ever about the overall worth of BBC sports coverage. Those who do control the purse strings at the BBC were faced with a difficult choice when joint contracts with Sky ended: to secure rights to live FA Cup ties and the final or Premiership highlights for *Match of the Day*. Des reckoned: 'I'd like to have my cake and eat it, but if there was to be a choice I think they got it right. If they couldn't afford both, *Match of the Day* was the one to go for. It's something regular, something that viewers associate with us, part of the history of sports television.'

BBC executives defend their sports department with vigour. A BBC spokesman told me:

'It is curious that other broadcasters "lose" sports rights to the BBC and it doesn't rate a mention. For example, Channel Four lost athletics to BBC Sport last year. It is inevitable that some contracts will move to other broadcasters as more and more outlets become available. It is a long time since the BBC was the only option and, of course, had rights to everything. But it would be wrong to suggest or imply that the BBC was in any way complacent or didn't care.

'We know that it is an ever more competitive world and we are prepared to face that competition and fight for any sports rights which suit our strategy. The facts are that only five contracts have moved in six years. BBC Sport signs around fifteen television sports contracts every year –

many against stiff competition from commercial rivals. An example of that is the US Masters golf.

'There is a great deal of misinformation and hysteria about the BBC and sport. The fact, again, is that our sports coverage is expanding in most areas, the multi-media sports department is thriving and we provide a breadth of sports coverage unequalled anywhere on terrestrial television. The biggest regular sports programmes are all on BBC – radio and television. By far the biggest majority of people follow Premiership football on BBC television through *Match of the Day*. That's five to six million people forty weeks a year.

'Of course, losing the Cup Final was a blow because it was an event we would like to have retained and we worked hard to do so, but were outbid in this instance by ITV. It doesn't mean that the contract has gone for ever.

'As for the Champions League, ITV has a strategy of cherry-picking a few sports which suit the profile required by its advertisers. It then puts in a massive bid, putting the rights beyond the purse of other broadcasters. This it has done with both the Champions' League and Formula One Grand Prix. This is no criticism of ITV – it is simply their strategy to broadcast about four sports whereas the BBC broadcasts around fifty, being a public service broadcaster.

'BSkyB is a totally different business to the BBC. It is a subscription business which relies on one or two ratings certainties to encourage people to take out subscriptions. Sky chose football and movies as its self-confessed "battering ram". Again, no criticism of Sky – it is a perfectly acceptable commercial strategy.

'So, Sky opted to spend around £700 million on "live" football. Bear in mind that Sky has three dedicated sports channels, several dedicated movie channels and not a lot else apart from purchased programmes like *Friends*, *The X Files* and *Star Trek*, which are then endlessly repeated. And this on roughly the same income as the BBC which provides multiple general interest television channels; five national radio networks, countless local radio stations; the biggest European internet site, and so on.

'The BBC originates most of its programmes – Sky buys cheap imports. We have an obligation as a public service broadcaster to offer programming that appeals to the widest possible audience – both in sport and in general. Sky does not have such a requirement – and give little back to the British economy by way of taxes either!'

One consequence of this ever-fiercer battle for broadcasting rights was the axing of *Sportsnight*, which Des presented in 1996. *Sportsnight* had been around for thirty years and had a wider remit than *Match of the Day*. But losing Formula One, the FA Cup, Test Cricket and the Ryder Cup forced the BBC into a rethink.

In regard to the wider world of sport, Des also knows that to a large extent it's not the BBC's fault that prime events are being lost to terrestrial television and, therefore, to the vast majority of potential viewers. And he's quick to take up the cudgels on behalf of the ordinary fan. When England internationals went to Sky, he said:

'The FA made that decision. They went for the money. Then they start yelling that isn't it a shame you can't see live England games on terrestrial television. They should have thought about that when they did the deal in the first place.

'I'd like to question the other sports bodies who sell their products, like the Ryder Cup, to Sky television. They don't understand that the event belongs to the nation, or the European people, and the event is diminished because it's hidden away. Surely it shouldn't be just about money with these events.'

His battles to save the flagship *Match of the Day* were never about money. Timing was the issue which Des believed posed the greatest threat. At its peak, *Match of the Day* pulled in around ten million viewers – that was in 1972 – but now it's just half of that. At one point it dropped to a disastrous 3.8 million, although figures rallied back towards the five million mark.

Des fought for an earlier time slot, saying: 'The programme is on far too late, it's as simple as that. The BBC know I think this and I've taken the argument to the highest levels. They all know how I feel. The best figures we ever had were when it went out earlier, around ten o'clock. How many of us want to start watching a programme starting at 10.50 pm. It's in the land of nodding off.' He eventually partially won the battle when the BBC started to screen the show at 10.30 pm in 1998.

When the show was starting at 10.50 and finishing after midnight, Des made his point by wishing viewers a 'Good morning' as he signed off. He campaigned long and loud around the corridors of the BBC for a better slot and was certainly responsible for getting the programme repeated on a Sunday morning. He used to complain: 'What grieves me most is that we are losing young people. I get letters galore from parents complaining that their children want to stop up until midnight to watch it. People here say the children can always video it.'

A BBC spokesman says:

'*Match of the Day* was originally earlier in the evening on BBC2 but since it moved to BBC1 it has always been the first programme after the peak Saturday night hours. Research shows that it achieves a maximum audience at that time because fans who have travelled to matches are back home and those who have been out for the evening have returned.

'Scheduling is a very complex matter and there are other commitments on a Saturday evening. Then there is the evening news to be slotted in and *Match of the Day* has for a long time followed that news.'

Des had been bringing football into British homes, forty weeks of the year – always from the very best seat in the house – since 1988. The *Match of the Day* viewpoint is considered to be the finest available, and not just by the armchair fans who love to watch the highlights and analysis, swept along, of course, by Des's sparkling links and pithy observations. No, some of the biggest fans of this sporting institution are the players themselves. And they all recognize one thing: Des is the fans' man! His replacement in the hot seat will certainly know he's got a hard act to follow.

Former Arsenal and England soccer international Ian Wright made a memorable appearance on *Match of the Day* on New Year's Day 1997 – and he was clearly almost as excited about it as appearing in a cup final. Wright sat in for ex-Liverpool ace Alan Hansen just a few hours after scoring his two hundredth League goal in Arsenal's 2–0 win over Middlesbrough. He says:

'When I went on the *Match of the Day* panel I just said to Des, "Man, this is my Graceland . . ." because it was. I had been watching *Match of the Day* ever since I was a kid, all through growing up, and to actually be on it, on the panel, was brilliant.

'And I was with Des and Des is the man, you know. Des is the nuts, for want of a better word.'

Even Des was taken aback with Wright's obvious pleasure at being invited onto the panel. He says: 'Ian was obviously chuffed to be there. He had a schoolboy grin on his face throughout and he was a pleasure to have on the show.'

The famous Lynam wit was sharp as ever, however, when asked what he thought about the footballer's reference to *Match of the Day* as his 'Graceland'. 'It was clearly a reference to Elvis's place,' said Des, 'but I didn't know if he perhaps meant I was dead.'

In the months after his impressive showing on *Match of the Day*, Ian Wright began to get more offers of television work, culminating in his own chat show. But he still thinks everyone can learn from the master of broadcasting. He says: 'Des is the man. I think everybody likes Des. He has got the style, he's got the wit, he's got everything really.

'I remember Gary Lineker saying, "He's the ultimate, he's the best there is. Ever." '

Wright arrived for our meeting fresh from training with his latest club, West Ham. Fittingly as he paves the way for a future career in television when his playing days are over, we meet in the Groucho Club in London's Soho – watering hole of the capital's media movers and shakers. Wright is promoting his latest TV venture – a compilation of squirmingly squeamish human feats from the *Guinness World of Records*. He already knows how hard it can be leaping the gulf from being a guest on a show to being the presenter of it, and acknowledges that no one does it better than Des.

'I had done a few interviews and things leading into TV which got me used to the camera, but what does catch you out more than anything else is when you have got a live crowd there. You don't know what they are going to do, you don't know what they are going to say.

'Sometimes the least little distraction can just completely throw you and those are the things you have to get used to. You just have to be very focused. You have to learn.

'Des is just so professional and he's so cool and calm on air. Even if something went completely, catastrophically wrong he would still be in charge. That's the secret. Des obviously does his homework, too, that's why he can be so relaxed and cool.

'You can't really try to be like Des or to match up to Des – but I'm going to try and work hard to beat him.'

Big Breakfast presenter Johnny Vaughan, whose own future as a television icon is assured, reckons that Des transcends the barriers of age, fashion and class. He says: 'Nobody can make a studio look as comfortable as Des. As long as he is there you know that nothing can go wrong. He performs a choric role and he is such a believable sports fan. He is the master of the raised eyebrow and there's a wryness and subtlety to his act.'

Though he has presented *Grandstand* and *Sportsnight*, it is *Match of the Day* for which Des became best known.

Des, in fact, took over the *Match of the Day* reins from Jimmy Hill who remained a regular guest on the programme until the start of 1999 when he offered his services to Sky television. At the time, the BBC only had rights to cover FA Cup matches but the return of a full *Match of the Day* programme in 1992 brought joy to millions of soccer-holics. As anchorman, Des often watched with undisguised amusement over the years as the sparks flew between, maybe, Hill and Alan Hansen. Or, more memorably, between Hill and the former England coach Terry Venables. It used to be the one question he got asked more than any other: 'Do Jimmy Hill and Terry Venables really dislike each other?' As you would expect, Des would only ever give a diplomatic answer.

Certainly, he had a reputation on the programme for putting people in their place – with subtlety and good humour – if they ever became too pompous. On one occasion Jimmy Hill was relating events from way back in history when he told viewers: 'I was employed by the BBC even then, in a minor capacity, of course.' Quick as a flash, Des retorted: 'You're still in a minor capacity, Jimmy.'

Des also admits to having a quiet word off-air with one or two of the more forthright players and managers who have passed through the studio as panellists. He recalls: 'We had one panellist during the 1986 World Cup who kept making jokes about the surnames of foreign players. I did say to him, "Well, your name would probably sound a bit ridiculous to them." '

The very first *Match of the Day* kicked off in black and white on BBC2 in 1964, featuring Liverpool, who were the defending league champions, against their old rivals Arsenal. England World Cup hero Roger Hunt knocked in the first goal for the Merseyside outfit as they battled to a 3–2 victory. With Kenneth Wolstenholme – two years before his immortal World Cup winning comment from 1966 – in the presenter's chair, the programme was something of a nervous experiment for the BBC, who were testing the technological advances of electronic cameras and videotape to the limits.

That first broadcast attracted just 20,000 viewers – less than half the number of people who watched the game live at Anfield. But, as they say, from little acorns . . . . Wolstenholme remained in the hot seat until 1967 when David Coleman took over. Barry Davies sat in for a few shows between 1972 and 1973, although Coleman didn't officially hand over the chair to Jimmy Hill until 1973. Hill, who joined the BBC from ITV, remained in the post – often outraging viewers with his forthright opinions – until Des arrived on the scene in 1988. Hill had former Arsenal and Scotland goalkeeper Bob Wilson as his right-hand man and sometime presenter of the programme, a role Bob carried on after Des's arrival.

A few memorable moments along the way which football fans will cherish gives the flavour of the programme's heritage: the World Cup triumph of 1966 put *Match of the Day* into a peak-time slot on BBC1 and watching the programme started to become a Saturday night ritual. On 15 November 1969, the show reached another broadcasting milestone when a game between Liverpool and West Ham became the first league match in Britain to be shown in colour. And in 1970 the first Goal of the Month competition was won by Coventry's Ernie Hunt with the cheekiest of goals after Willie Carr flicked up the ball with his heels in a 'donkey kick' which he copied from a Brazilian.

The show introduced trial by television in 1971 when a new invention called the video disc allowed slow-motion replay for the first time. And it couldn't have been put to more controversial use. Leeds United lost 1–0 to West Bromwich Albion, a defeat which cost them the championship. But the Leeds players, coaching staff and, more importantly, the whole crowd were incensed because Albion's Colin Suggett was offside when Tony Brown picked up a rebound and headed towards goal. The linesman flagged and the Leeds defence stood still while Brown squared the ball to Jeff Astle who scored the game's only goal. The referee, however, decided that the offside player was not interfering with play and, with great understatement, commentator Barry Davies proclaimed, 'Leeds will go mad.'

The resulting pitch invasion meant that Leeds had to play the first four home games of the following season away from home on a neutral ground. Back in the studio, the team were able to analyse the incident with the benefit of the replays and judge that the referee acted perfectly correctly.

Such was the popularity of the show, Cardinal Basil Hume,

the Archbishop of Westminster and leader of the nation's Roman Catholics, revealed during an interview on *Grandstand* that he was a mad-keen Newcastle United fan and wanted the *Match of the Day* theme tune to be played at his funeral. Unfortunately, in keeping with the sombre nature of the occasion, his request was not fulfilled after his death in 1999. Only the most dedicated trivia buff would know that the famous music was composed by a man named Barry Stroller and that it was introduced just after the 1970 World Cup. Any attempts to tinker with the musical accompaniment to the show's opening credits have been met with fierce opposition – including a complaint lodged in the House of Commons.

The programme's twenty-first anniversary celebrations in 1985 went unnoticed as disaster engulfed the game of soccer. The terrible fire at Bradford on 11 May 1985 and then the Heysel disaster in Brussels during a European Cup Final between Liverpool and Juventus signalled a bleak time for the game, with smaller crowds and behind-the-scenes wrangles over television rights. Domestic football disappeared from the screen until January 1986 and with general disenchantment over recorded league highlights, Saturday night league soccer vanished for seven years. The programme's Silver Jubilee in 1989 was overshadowed by another tragedy – the appalling disaster at Hillsborough, Sheffield, which set in motion a train of events which would change the face of football forever.

The Hillsborough disaster was Europe's worst-ever soccer tragedy. Ninety-four football fans were crushed to death and more than two hundred people injured as fans flooded into the ground for the FA Cup semi-final between Liverpool and Nottingham Forest. *Match of the Day* that night carried no football – just eyewitness accounts of the terrible events that unfolded on 15 April 1989. Of course, all the *Match of the Day* team were moved by the horror of it all. Des, who had experience of reporting from a major tragedy when the Israeli athletes were murdered during the Munich Olympics, was as grief-stricken as the rest.

Des had actually gone to the game with Jimmy Hill and he watched horrified as events beyond anyone's control unfolded.

Des was due to present *Match of the Day* that night but he and Jimmy had decided to watch the game live rather than on monitors back in the studio. There would be plenty of time, they reckoned, to make it back to London in time to present the show.

The traumatic events began when thousands of supporters headed into an already over-crowded terrace at the Leppings Lane end of Hillsborough, where the Liverpool support had been concentrated. Just minutes after the game kicked off there was a surge as supporters poured into the ground desperate to get inside to see the match. The dead and injured were crushed against security fencing or were buried under falling bodies after crush barriers gave way. Sadly, many of the dead and injured were children who had gone to the front, against the security fencing, to get a better view.

By the time the authorities realized what was happening, it was too late and supporters began tearing down the security fence and ripping up perimeter hoardings to use as makeshift stretchers.

Brian Barwick, a Liverpudlian and former Head of Sport at the BBC, says:

'I was editor of *Match of the Day* at the time. I am also from Merseyside, and I am also a Liverpool supporter, so the whole day and the whole programme rang with resonance for me.

'I would think that was probably the most memorable broadcast that I have been involved with and therefore I would suggest that it is also high on Desmond's list of notable programmes.

'He and Jimmy Hill, who were due to appear on the programme, had actually gone up to see the game first hand. So, in the end, they did see the difficulties first hand.

'To be editor of *Match of the Day* that night . . . it was just a sad moment. It was the only edition where we've had no football at all. We just talked to eyewitnesses about the events of the day. But it was important that the programme was carried, because the tragedy was in the hearts and souls of football fans.'

Bob Wilson, who had been on the *Grandstand* team that afternoon, recalls:

'It was such a terrible, terrible thing to see. It was the most difficult thing I have ever had to deal with.

'Throughout it all, I had to keep the programme going. We were covering the World Snooker Championships at the Crucible in Sheffield and then going back to Hillsborough, saying, "Here's the latest from John Motson or whoever," but the problem was that we knew very quickly that there were dead bodies.

'They were putting them outside our BBC scanner, but we could not say anything about them, because it could have caused a panic. There were still so many people in the ground. So, we had to keep the programme going when there were increasing numbers of fatalities and it was becoming clear that there was a major incident. It got more and more difficult to do it.

'At the end of the programme I had to say that there had been fatalities, and I remember choosing the words carefully, saying: 'If you are worried about any of your family or loved ones . . .'

In the aftermath of the tragedy, Lord Justice Taylor's detailed report into football grounds and safety at football matches resulted in sweeping changes. Stadiums were modernized and made all-seaters. the game was dragged into the twentieth century – just in time for the dawn of the twenty-first century.

That, then, is a brief history of *Match of the Day*. But what about the programme itself? Des says:

'Niall Sloane [editor of the programme], principally, with some influence from me, will select who we might like to interview at the games. It won't necessarily be the guy who scores two goals, but it might be the guy who played particularly well in midfield. We will look at the game and decide on, maybe, the manager and a couple of players.

The manager is the easy option but it is better to get an articulate player who has something to say.'

From 6.00 pm onwards, the editing team are busy producing a smooth version of the game which fits its allotted time slot. The skill is to keep the flow of the game without any obvious jumps where footage has had to be cut. All kick-offs, half-times and the final whistle must be kept in the final edit. The biggest nightmare can be getting the sound right, though. Says one BBC editor:

'Sound can be an unknown quantity. Four-letter words can be fired off by players in the heat of the battle, or the crowd are swearing, or you pick it up from someone on the bench.

'But for the editing team the biggest problem can occur when there's a goal. If, say, it's a penalty and the crowd are shouting "The referee's a xxxxxx" it is all mixed in with the general crowd roar. You can't substitute that bit of noise with something from when the ball was in midfield because it's a goal – it just wouldn't work. You just have to do the best you can.'

Des finds a quiet corner and sits down to write his introduction and conclusion pieces and the links between matches and analysis. 'It's pretty tightly scripted,' he says. 'We might discard what you might call the statistical opening and do something where the directors have picked out different pictures, or nice themes if we're lucky. Obviously the chat is off the top of one's head to a large degree, although that too is dictated by what videotape they want to get in.'

By the time the show begins, the edited tapes, graphics and music are all in place and it's time for the presenters to shine.

Des is like the fans' representative in the midst of the professional sportsmen. He says what you and I would like to say, asks the questions we would like to ask.

'Well, that's what I like to think the viewers think,' says Des. ' "Des will put our questions and those footballers won't get away with it if they talk gobbledegook".'

Now Des is bringing his vast experience and insight into what those viewers really *do* want, to ITV rather than the BBC. *Match of the Day* will be poorer for the loss of Des but no one could deny that, finally, he was left with no choice but to accept ITV's offer.

They had pushed the boat out to secure the big games. Now they've brought on board the biggest of the big names. Desmond Lynam is catch of the day.

Epilogue

It was 1969 when an extremely nervous Des Lynam kissed his wife, Susan, and said, 'Wish me luck,' before leaving home in Brighton for his first day as a radio reporter with the BBC.

Des was following in the footsteps of the great Eamonn Andrews, who started as a boxing reporter before becoming a household name. He was racked by self-doubt and the fear of falling flat on his face – just like most young professionals faced with taking a giant step up the career ladder. A leap into the unknown, their own abilities as yet unproven.

Des knew his stuff, though. At his interview he was handed a list of forty sporting questions and amazed the BBC panel by getting thirty-nine correct. And that was it, Des was flying. Within six months he was offered the presenter's seat on *Sports Report* and another BBC legend was in the making.

He could have had no idea at the time, not the slightest inkling, just how famous he would become. Almost exactly thirty years later, Des walked out of the doors at Broadcasting House for the last time – a national treasure and the most instantly recognizable face in sport on British television.

Quite ironically his shock decision to quit for a lucrative new job over on ITV occurred in the run-up to another momentous event – the last total eclipse of the millennium. For weeks the country had been in the grip of eclipse fever, with soothsayers and astrologists predicting all manner of disquieting conse-quences. Some warned that the blotting out of the sun by the moon presaged the end of the world. By the time it came around, there were some at the BBC who really did think it had ended. One thing was for sure, all the babble and talk about it being a 'time of change' was spot on in Des's case.

He said he felt stale after hundreds of *Match of the Day* programmes, numerous Grand Nationals, six Olympic Games and anchoring countless other sporting fixtures and events. If he was feeling jaded, he never let it show on screen. This was the man who had guided us through sporting triumphs and catastrophes with equal aplomb. We'd been to enough World Cups and European football and athletics championships with Des to know if he was getting screen fatigue, surely?

The BBC tried gamely to smile through the humiliating defection of their biggest presentational asset. Head of Sport Bob Shennan said he was disappointed, but some bitterness was evident in his description of Des's decision being a personal choice 'at this late stage in his career'.

He added: 'I think he would be the first person to say that no presenter is bigger than BBC Sport as a whole.'

Quite true. But Des's experience and achievements do make him a particularly dazzling star in the somewhat characterless television firmament. Let's not just consider his calm authority and ability to handle tricky situations during fast-changing live events. Des could have been the man who invented the slogan 'We won't make a drama out of a crisis'.

No, Des's real achievement in television has been to make the watching public feel part of the event, part of the team. He introduced humour and a common touch to arenas which had previously been either frantic or elitist. David Coleman, for all his bubbling genius and enthusiasm, could never have endeared himself to the non-sporting public the way Des has done. Wimbledon could have remained a cool, aloof event rather than a real people's tournament without the laconic touches brought to the BBC's coverage by Des and his former co-host Gerry Williams. And who else would defy the 'party line' approach of those who consider every Olympic event as sacrosanct and deadly serious to tell us: 'Going down to the pub is not yet an Olympic sport. But beach volleyball is.'

With Des you know he's not going to try to 'sell' an event to you. Now that he's left the BBC he might try to sell us a few more products, on top of Miracle Gro fertilizer and Right Guard antiperspirant, but at least we know the difference between adverts and programmes. The point about Des is that he has never tried to say, 'Hey, get a load of this, it's going to be brilliant' when he knows that a mid-table battle in the mud of mid-winter Nottingham is likely to be about as exciting as matchstick model-making. He also brought charm and integrity along with the humour and the firm grasp in his own mind of the place sport holds in the greater scheme of things. It can't always have been easy.

Along the way he has faced battles over his style and approach but he always stuck to his guns – never more so than in his long-running skirmishes with BBC management over the scheduling of *Match of the Day*. He's the fans' man. The people's champion. One of us.

Des himself puts his transition from fairly well known presenter to household name down to the Olympic Games of 1984, when sports fans started to notice that they actually enjoyed the coverage of an event just that little bit more when Des Lynam was presenting it. His catchphrases began to work their way into our psyche and his deft raising of an eyebrow could convey a thousand words about any particular incident. Now, *that's* the Lynam magic.

His decision to take what his old friend and new boss, Brian Barwick, Head of ITV Sport, describes as 'his special style of presentation' across London from Shepherds Bush to Gray's Inn Road, caused shockwaves throughout sport. It happened after seventy-two hours of intense negotiations which took place four weeks after the ITV offer was first put to Des.

To those lamenting the BBC's accelerating loss of both product and personalities, across the board not just in sport, there was something inevitable about it all. For Des it marked a step in many ways as eventful as the one which took him out of the 'amateur' days of local radio and into the heart of the world's leading broadcasting authority all those years ago. Now, as then, it was not an easy decision to make.

But with the fresh challenge of his new ITV role and the prospect of more exciting commercial opportunities ahead, Des enters the new millennium on a personal high.

His salary now matches his status as the nation's Number One sports presenter, and he is even rumoured to be interested in buying a palatial £2 million penthouse flat in a development in which Harrod's boss Mohamed Al Fayed and Liverpool soccer captain Jamie Redknapp would be his neighbours.

As Des says: 'It's no secret that live football is what I love best. The chance to anchor ITV's peaktime Champions League coverage as well as the FA Cup and other major football was just too tempting to turn down. And to cap it all, I will now also have time to watch my beloved Brighton and Hove Albion play again, back in their home town.'

Tell you what, Des . . . You deserve it.